The Awakening

Living an Enchanted Life in a Disenchanted World

Dr Colm O'Connor

Gill & Macmillan

Gill & Macmillan
Hume Avenue
Park West
Dublin 12
www.gillmacmillanbooks.ie

978 07171 6394 6

Print origination by Carole Lynch
Printed and bound by ScandBook AB, Sweden

'Come to the Edge' by Christopher Logue, copyright
© Christopher Logue, 1969

This book is typeset in Adobe Garamond 12pt.

*The paper used in this book comes from the wood
pulp of managed forests. For every tree felled, at least
one tree is planted, thereby renewing natural resources.*

A CIP catalogue record for this book is available
from the British Library.

5 4 3 2 1

Acknowledgements

I am indebted to a number of people who have facilitated this book. My late father embodied so much of what is written in these pages. His love of Irish literature, art, poetry, Celtic mythology and culture still, many years after his death, inspires my efforts. I miss him greatly but his silent encouragement runs through the spine of this book. My mother, now in her eighties, lives day by day the enchantment and ever-cheerful heroism I write about in this book. I am continually inspired by her grace and wisdom.

My special thanks and love to my wife Jean, whose patience and encouragement over the past two years has made possible so much of my early morning, sleep-disturbing writing. Her unquestioning encouragement and support of my efforts have been humbling and I dedicate this work to her.

This book came together through my many hours of conversation with my brother, Gerry, over a few pints every Thursday night at Tracey's Bar in Ballincollig, County Cork. We quickly discovered that we shared a similar feeling for what keeps us buoyant and hopeful in a life that is often painful and depressing. We talked about how we strive to live an awakened life in a stress-filled world and how we can rise above all manner of difficult situations by way of imagination, perspective and what I call 'Mind-Flight'. Our conversations inspired a great deal of this book and I am indebted to Gerry for his continued companionship and perceptiveness throughout this journey.

My three children, Brendan, Christine and Ciara, animate my life in ways they will never know and they are the inspiration for many of these reflections. Ciara's innate spirituality, at the age of 11, delights me. Brendan's courage and optimism inspire me and Christine's steadfastness and character reassure me.

I am indebted to Eoin O'Flynn, who read an initial draft of this book and was inspiring in his encouragement of my efforts. He is one of the enchanted people who has illuminated my life.

My colleagues at the CMCC, Paul Street have been a deep well from which I have drawn so much and are part of the hidden life-sustaining narrative behind this book.

My thanks to all the staff at Gill & Macmillan, who have played such a significant part in the stewardship of this book through its many stages, especially Deirdre Nolan, who believed in it from the outset.

Finally, I have been greatly influenced by my Irish heritage. My Celtic origins have percolated up through the soil of my being and influenced the feeling of this book. My character has been shaped by my history, my place, my name and my roots. The landscape and countryside where I write is littered with ancient sites, standing stones, forts, stone circles, symbols and stories that, unlike any other place on Earth, give us a unique perspective on the questions posed by life. Such culture, symbols and spirituality give us something that psychology and psychiatry never can.

Contents

'This was altogether new. I loved the crafting of words, the sense of "floating over" and the idea of the burning point of life. It awakens me to the beauty on this detour called life I am privileged to be on.'

Fr Brian Conlon, The Family Centre, Boyle

'This was very inspiring stuff that awakened the gift that life is, how we take so much for granted and need to create space for awe.'

Bernadette Ryan, Relationship Psychotherapist, Dublin

'I loved the approach to the awesome reality of being human. The beauty of the vertical life touched into my own spiritual journey.'

Ann Prendergast, Gestalt Psychotherapist, Co. Waterford

'I really enjoyed this material and how Mind-Flight is the way we rise above and see things in perspective.'

Pamela Roche, Counsellor, Dublin

'This has moved me greatly and onto my vertical plane. The necessity of enchantment to deal with reality was brilliant and the difference between my vertical and horizontal self was great. I loved the language and the use of words.'

Joan McCarrick, Biologist, Sligo

'It was very inspiring and I loved every moment – particularly the celebration of our ancient history and the image of the Celtic Cross.'

Leonie Gallagher, Psychotherapist, Dublin

'I found this very stimulating and provoking and also felt at peace. I loved the ideas of heroism and enchantment and the use of the image of the Celtic Cross.'

Dr Maeve Hurley, Director of Ag Eisteacht, Cork

Prologue

The Skelligs

Twelve miles off the coast of West Kerry stands one of the wonders of the world. Skellig Michael is one of two striking rocks that rise up out of the Atlantic Ocean like mountain peaks breaking the surface of the world. Seen by the fortunate who have taken the local boats from Portmagee or Derrynane, the ancient monastic settlement on Skellig Michael is an astonishing example of the imagination and heroism of the first monks of early Christian Ireland.

During my childhood our family went to west Kerry every summer; my parents used to rent a caravan by Glenbeg beach near Caherdaniel. It was perched on the sandy grass facing Kenmare Bay and the magnificent mountains of the Beara Peninsula. Seven of us piled into a five-person caravan, from which were created the wonderful memories of childhood: bare feet for the summer, sleeping bags at night, the comfort of parents' conversations as we drifted into sleep, the sound of waves in the background, swimming daily in the wild Atlantic, the smell of fresh mackerel, gas lights at night and the feeling of being enveloped by Creation in a safe and mysterious world.

Every few days my father would drive us the 11 miles to Waterville to stretch the eyes and limbs beyond the confines of our small abode. The car wound its way above the splendour of Derrynane Harbour through the mountain pass 800 feet above the sea. At the pass stood a large stone statue of the Virgin Mary with arms outstretched as if guiding us through, as the road opened up to the breathtaking vista of Ballinskelligs Bay and the sprinkled white specks of little houses along its coastline.

As you wind down along the cliff edge the scenery opens up and there is a point where the majestic Skellig rocks come into view for the first time, beyond the whale-like profile of Bolus Head in the distance. Coming up to this point my father would slow down and tell us to wait in anticipation until they came into view and say, as he did on a hundred other journeys through the pass, 'Look at the Skelligs. Look,' and he'd ask, 'Can you see them?' Always my father would point out their splendour, describe them with his artist's eye and prompt us to feel a sense of the sacred in our natural world.

The larger Skellig rock was the home of the early monks who went to live there in about AD 580. They chose what would appear to be the most inhospitable place in Ireland. They built stone beehive-shaped huts on small outcrops of rock and soil 600 feet above the sea, where any missed step could send them to their death in the raging swell of sea and rocks below. That these were places where these monks went to meditate, live, pray and write is nothing short of astonishing.

Those amazing pilgrims chose to find their God at the wildest and most isolated point of nature as they began a movement in Ireland that lasted almost 800 years.

For me as a child, the Skelligs were not just another breathtaking scene but a vision that evoked a sense of wonder at the invisible life that lay beyond the world I knew. These kinds of places draw something from the human heart that nothing else can. They resonate with something ancient in the soul and get us to half-remember something about who we are. Nature does this to us too. The natural world invites you towards it; it welcomes you and reminds you of things you have forgotten.

As inspirational as any great religious site, the Skelligs represent the unique character of both our Celtic and early Christian heritage before we were subject to invasions from Scandinavia, Europe and Britain. In contrast to the dark themes of Nordic or German myths, scholars have noted that Irish legends, myths and rituals from this early era are often uplifting, with a hopeful message that promised a means of rising above the challenges and dangers of life. Alongside the brutalities of life, the Irish had in fact developed a mystical light-heartedness.

Inspired by our shared Celtic legacy, this book attempts to show how we can recultivate that lightness of heart that rises from the weight of the world and live an 'enchanted life'.

Introduction

Most of us try to think our way through life. We spend our days problem solving, investing all our energies contemplating and attempting to remove the obstacles that seem to impede our progress. We think that peace or perfection is achieved by looking more closely at our problems rather than looking more expansively at ourselves. We think our purpose is to be rational, to deal with everyday reality and address sequentially the problems it presents to us. Yet if this small, rational view is our only reference point, we get stressed, depressed and anxious.

Amazingly, however, we are not supposed to be rational beings. We actually never were rational beings. We were always so much more than that. Taken to its extreme, rationalism creates a form of psychological autism; we become champions of details and literal reality, but alienated from the meaning and experience of existence itself. When we seek to control reality our worldview becomes constrictive and rigid. In this kind of world, playfulness, good cheer, imagination, transcendence, genuine joy and compassion find it hard to get any purchase and any sense of spirituality in our lives becomes diminished.

What the ancient Irish give us is the courage to build our spirituality facing, like the monks on the Skelligs, straight into the wild, majestic and at times brutal realities of life. This kind of fearless psychology offers an inspiration that is unique in the world. And, like the teeming bird life on the sanctuary of Little Skellig, we can take flight and be held aloft by the very gales that threatened to blow us away.

The Celtic Cross

It is the ancient Irish who gave us the Celtic Cross; and throughout this book the Celtic Cross is used as a metaphor for how we can live an integrated, vibrant life. The vertical axis of the cross is taken to represent our 'Vertical Self' – the elevated, symbolic, vulnerable, soulful self that looks to the stars and experiences the unadorned bliss of just being alive, senses the temporality and preciousness of life and uses the magic of the imagination to endure with good cheer and confidence. The cross's horizontal axis represents our matter-of-fact Horizontal Self – the literal realist who observes physical reality, has a clinical, logical take on things and feels the stress and anxiety of life as it is day to day. It can be easy today to become trapped in this Horizontal Self, but to live fully, we need to occupy the point where these two axes intersect – at what I call the 'burning point'. We must attend to both the Horizontal and the Vertical Self, but the Vertical Self must be allowed to triumph because it brings reality in from the cold to the warmth of an enchanted life. The Celtic Cross, then, is a metaphor for how we can keep a foot in both the mundane and the marvellous.

The Essentials of Life

Mind-Flight

The ability of the mind to fly – 'mind-flight' – is at the heart of this book. It is the ability of the mind to elevate itself above circumstance and give life a glorious meaning. It is the defining human characteristic that has enabled not only the development of culture, civilisation and art, but, more important, it has allowed ordinary people to rise to the occasion of life itself and make something magical out of the mundane. This legacy of our Celtic past is a kind of spiritual alchemy for humankind.

In this way, the book reveals the magnificent and inspirational efforts of people everywhere to raise themselves up from anonymity to be somebody, from the girl at the checkout who lightens your load with good cheer, to the refugee carrying her infant child across some mountain border. Heroism, with a small 'h', is to be seen everywhere you look – all of it without applause or recognition. If we took it all in we would be awe-struck by the courage of each solitary soul in this beautiful life.

Hope

One question at the core of this book is this: When all else is lost, what is it that we hold on to? What is it that sustains us? It is hope. And why, unlike all other animals in creation, do humans need hope? The answer to this question reveals the most inspiring truth we know, and it is at the heart of this book.

This book is inspired by the courage and imagination of people who find hope where there appears to be none, purpose where there appears to be little and joy in what appears to be grim. Everywhere people do something with their life that is magical, awesome and redemptive. People live out a small heroic life in which they find hope and meaning in that which appears to be hopeless, in which they strive optimistically for something they cannot quite get. They elevate their life to something heroic and purposeful, each person *trying* to be something more than what they are. Everywhere people are gathering fragments of heaven from the debris of life. The effort everywhere of people trying to be more than what they are is a quite astonishing and inspiring human enterprise.

This book is not a self-help book that tells you what to do; rather, it is a personal development book – a series of reflections, inspired by Celtic mythology and spirituality, which may encourage you to 'be' in the world in a different way. I wrote it for myself as much as anyone because I too struggle to see things differently, to get the big picture. If the melody and tone of what I try to say can be heard beneath the words, maybe I will have succeeded. If this touches your heart, then we have connected, because I too wear the garment of sorrow that is part of living. My hope is that you find me a companion as we walk through the landscape of the human heart, perhaps seeing different things but sharing the same poetic imagination.

The Macroscopic View

In a world dominated by rationalism, an overarching sense of our common humanity is needed today more than ever. We do not need more specialisation, which fragments societies and communities; rather, we need a general way to understand and integrate all of the broken pieces of our life. We need to see how the hundreds of problems people have in life are all the same universal problem dressed up in different clothes. This book takes this view and resists the errors of specialisation.

If you want to understand why you do what you do there are two ways in which you can examine your own life. One is to look closely at the details of your life and try to figure out what you need to do in order to make a difference. This is the microscopic approach. The other approach is macroscopic; you see your life in the context of the full breadth of the human condition. Just as a microscope is great for observing small things but useless if you want to see the stars, rationality is useful for figuring out your current bank balance, but is useless for figuring out how you want to live life. Being an intelligent and rational person is good for many things, but as a guidebook for life it can only get you so far. To go further you need the macroscopic view – to see your life in the round, to experience a meaning that takes you beyond your problems.

The Awakening

In Chapter 2 I suggest that imagination began at the dawn of human self-consciousness – a moment I call the awakening; that is, the point at which we became aware that we exist and that at some time we will die. It was clear that the shock of this awareness triggered a state of emergency for humankind. For every positive consequence associated with being aware that one is alive there was a negative consequence in being aware that one will also die. So the awakening was the stirring of the opposites of awe and dread, of gratitude and terror. It also triggered the need for people to counteract their helplessness by proving themselves in some way. What sprang forth from this existential awakening was imagination, which in turn begat what I call the provinces of enchantment. This effort became the fuel for both civilisation and personal heroism.

In Chapter 3 I point out that it is critical not to offer a prescription for the good or enchanted life without having the courage to look directly at why we need it in the first place and to take on board the degree to which terror and vulnerability lie at the core of our being. I could not present a book related to hope without embracing the hopelessness inherent in the human condition. Humankind's essential problem is that we want eternal life but are burdened with a mortal one; and hope is the means of transcending this conundrum.

In Chapters 1, 4 and 5 I suggest that ancient Irish mythology is a story not about facts but about our symbolic life. The stories of Irish mythology remind us that we inhabit not just a physical place, but an enchanted and magical inner landscape populated by metaphorical companions who walk with us. They remind us that we live by life-enhancing illusions not to escape reality but to engage with it fully. The enchanted life is one that turns the black and white world of reality to one of vivid colour and vibrant hope. Ancient Irish mythology reminds us that it was our original awakening that triggered this shift from a literal to a symbolic relationship with life from which there was no going back.

The Enchanted Life

I Part 2 I describe how the awakening of our helplessness and terror triggered what I call 'the enchanted life' and the quite magnificent human responses of imagination, transcendence, heroism, enchantment and poetry. These represented our refusal to accept reality and submit to life's relentlessness. Rather than succumbing to fate we began to respond to it.

These provinces are the sparkling jewels in the crown of thorns we call life. They represent the symbolic relationship that human beings developed with the world. Reality therefore became the arena, the dramatic stage where humanity acted out biblical themes and overcame them. For these reasons our relationship with the world became the stuff of myth. Our mythologies were descriptions of our relationship with reality and how we sought to resolve it. For that reason the ancient Irish legends of the Tuatha Dé Danann (the people of the goddess Danu) reveal this process of enchantment. They are reminders that beneath the surface of everyday life lie invisible forces, entities and resources that, if we harness them, can enhance our lives in profound ways.

History is the story of humanity's efforts to stretch up and out of its body to an imagined reality that awakened hope and possibility. I seek to describe in a robust way the place that enchantment, imagination and poetic intuition have in our everyday life. The poetic and imaginative quality of everyday life is rooted in our evolution and history and it is more than a tool for survival; it is a gateway to transcendence. The marginalisation of imagination and spirituality by modern myths of technology, progress, economics and science has many tragic consequences for us.

Enchantment and imagination are essential to our relationship with reality. Enchantment is not an avoidance strategy or some kind of artificial sweetener that makes life more palatable. It is the means by which we have to engage with the world. We are not just *in* the world, like unaware animals; we are *in relationship* with it, which is very different. We are ever so slightly separate from and above reality. The stuff of human life is therefore not external reality but our *relationship* with that reality. How we enchant the world is as invisible as electricity, gravity or light, but just as essential to a fulfilling life. Such a life is possible for us all. This book explores your relationship with your life and world and, as such, is an invitation to be the champion of your own awakening.

Part 1

The Awakening

Chapter 1

Beyond Mindfulness:
Ancient Ireland and You

B efore inviting you to look at yourself, I want to tickle your unconscious mind and connect you with your history – your roots in ancient Ireland. It is a connection that I hope you can keep alive so that when you think about your own 'little' life, you feel the sympathy of history in a way that means you do not feel quite so alone. The Celtic imagination and its unique sense of the sacred has the potential to allow you to 'fly' beyond the confines of our circumstances to something that gives you the courage to live in the here and now.

Go into any large bookshop today and you will find sections on both mindfulness and motivation: mindfulness as derived from the Eastern practice of meditation; and motivation borrowed from North American models of corporate success. We look to the East to figure out how to meditate. We look to the West to figure out how we can get what we want – be it money, relationships or success. In the same bookshop you will also find sections on philosophy, theology and psychology that all seem to emanate from Central Europe, where many of the great philosophers and psychologists were born. We have been hugely influenced by these external forces.

If instead of looking to the East, West or to Europe to find out how to stand, I believe more solid ground might be found at home. In Ireland we can perhaps access some eternal truths that have not been put through the sieve of European, Eastern or American influences. We have a unique history that reveals something about human nature and the soul that you do not find anywhere else in the world. And evidence of this history is everywhere in the Irish countryside, dotted as it is with the ruins of monasteries, stone circles and standing stones.

For thousands of years Ireland stood alone on the edge of the Atlantic Ocean, left to develop itself without colonisation or war, all of which came much later in its history. This isolation gave us something that no one else had. We could give to civilisation what no other nation could give: an ancient spirituality and wisdom born out of our undisturbed Neolithic, Celtic and early Christian civilisation, summed up in the cliché of being a nation of saints and scholars. Our faith, mythology, monasticism, literature, spirituality, history and poetry gave a unique sense of the sacred. In the records of ancient Ireland we find a hopeful psychology and spirituality that has something quite unique to offer.

Therefore we do not need to look west to the USA or east to Asia to learn how to meditate – our monks were pointing the way as far back as AD 500. Our own history of psychological spirituality offers something even more precious – not just mindfulness as practised by those early Irish monks, but also what I call 'Mind-Flight'. Mindfulness encourages us to live in the here and now. Celtic imagination, or Mind-Flight, encourages us to imagine the 'then' so that the 'now' has both meaning and passion.

Why Bother with Ancient Irish History?

The prehistoric Irish of the Mesolithic and Neolithic ages, the Celts and the early Christians were a bunch of mystics, monks and 'mad' heroes who prayed, sang and wrote the poetry of the 'Wild Atlantic' way of life. This book tries to honour that history and add some Celtic ingredients to our recipes for psychological relief. You might consider them spells of wisdom that have drifted in on the mist from the ancient peoples who inhabited our land, leaving signs and symbols that point the way back towards our essential nature.

Both the landscape and history of Ireland reveal something quite magnificent about how humanity has risen to the occasion of life itself. Our ancient history gives us images of our naked humanity before it was hidden beneath the robes of modern political civilisation. The footprints of the truth about our human purpose can be seen more clearly in the soil of ancient Ireland. This history is like a psychological archaeology site where we can excavate some essential truths about our emotional nature and identity – truths that can loosen the ties that bind us to the modern cults of technology, politics and economics.

Our countless megalithic monuments, our treasure house of Celtic mythology and legends and our early Christian monastic movement were all spontaneous creations of the human being who fronted up to life in its wild and most elemental forms. Each site, monument, myth, legend, incantation, monastery, poem or story bears within it some eternal truth about the human predicament and how we experience and ultimately transcend it. As a consequence of this, you inevitably find remnants of your own personal story buried in these ancient tombs of history.

We are drawn to our history and to our original identity not because of a curiosity about what things were like *back then* but because it evokes in us a realisation of who we are *right now*. Even if you don't know this, you feel it. To climb the steps of Skellig Michael, to drive along our Wild Atlantic Way, is to come home to a land of memories you cannot quite recall and be welcomed home by an invisible people who call your name. Our myths, legends, music and historic sites endure because they are about us as individual people. An Irish mythology binds all of our pre-Christian, Celtic and early monastic traditions. It awakens in each of us a subconscious personal mythology that guides and shapes our life.

Identity

If you want to know who you really are, imagine what you would be like if you were stripped of all the protective securities that surround you – your roles, responsibilities, financial security, state benefits, modern amenities and so on. Imagine what your real character would be if you were in some post-apocalyptic world and had lost everything except your very life. Would you be the same as you are now or would you crumble? Would something in you endure, or would you despair and collapse like cardboard in the rain? Would you rise to the occasion, as so many do in times of tragedy or catastrophe, or would you become a depressed or violent creature?

One way to try to answer this question is to examine how your ancestors coped with such situations. The human brain has changed very little over the past fifty thousand years. You and your ancestors are more similar than different. They did not have all of the securities provided by modern society, but their emotions, fears, hopes and longings were the same as yours. When you go back to the dawn of recorded history, before the development of institutional civilisation and colonisation, you can see yourself in all your psychological nakedness and dependency. This is a wonderful place to look for clues as to who you are as an individual and what we are as people. This is why our ancient history, our Celtic heritage and the influences of early Irish Christianity are windows to what we are really like.

If we strip you of the securities of our modern world and place you alongside your counterpart from Neolithic times, as if standing with them in any of the stone circles in Ireland, you will find that you both hunger for the same things: a feeling of significance, influence and belonging in the world.

Fortunately, we Irish have some of the oldest records of ancient times in the Western world. We have an extraordinarily rich fund of stories, legends and mythology that show us what we are really like. Ancient Ireland reveals aspects of our essential nature that are buried under the cloaks of modern comforts, securities and dependencies. We have much to learn from our ancestors and there are many noble human traits that progress, science and civilisation conceal but do not wash away.

It is vital that we do not consider ourselves to be different from these ancient people. We must not diminish the spiritual beliefs of our pre-Celtic, Celtic and early Christian ancestors. We are guided by the same stars and experience the same terror and awe in the face of Creation. When we look to ancient Ireland we discover that our desire, terrors and longings have not changed. We have the same intuition that we are part of something greater than our minds can comprehend and are carried by forces and powers beyond our grasp. Ancient Irish mythology is still alive in our language, place names, myths and legends, literature, monuments and, most of all, in the landscape of the earth, sea, mountains and sky that surround us. The deities that have been presumed to have decayed and died are still breathing within us.

A Celtic Psychology

The Neolithic, Celtic and early Christian psyche of the Irish was not infected by the Roman Empire as the rest of Europe was, and, apart from conflict-free immigration of people from

Britain and Europe, Ireland was left to its own devices until maybe the fifth century. This gave the Celtic spirit room to breathe and develop its own Irish character. Being grounded in native spirituality it took to monastic Christianity with the enthusiasm of all those who were hungry and ready for enlightenment.

The early Irish monks then took their monastic tradition of learning and meditation across Ireland, into Britain and out into Europe to trigger the emergence of Western civilisation after the Dark Ages. It was an amazing contribution to civilisation and psychological life and its legacy remains to this day. We invaded Europe not with a sword or the symbols of power, but with the spiritual symbols of silence, prayer, scholarship and mindfulness. This is all symbolised by Skellig Michael. This extraordinary rock and its monastic remains tell us about human nature, human imagination, the psycho-spiritual life of Irish people and the heroic and transcendent potential of humanity.

When you read any of my references to ancient Ireland I would ask that you also hear it as a metaphor for your own forgotten life. I recall examples from ancient history to remind you of your inner identity – how you are guided by a personal mythology more than by reason and that in a metaphoric way, you are influenced by the ancestral gods. I refer to Celtic spirituality, ancient history and our monastic heritage not as an example of what happened *back then* but really as a metaphor for what can happen now in the provinces of our inner life.

Chapter 2

The Awakening

The First Heartbeat of Self-consciousness: 'I Exist'

Let me take you back about a hundred thousand years, to the time when early humans walked the plains of Africa looking for food. Life expectancy was poor for these nomadic tribes and, just like the deer they hunted, when one of them died the rest of the tribe would carry on regardless, leaving the dead body behind them. As the tree does not grieve for its falling leaves, early humankind did not grieve for its dead. The human animal, like other creatures, kept on walking with scarcely a backward glance.

At a certain point, however, about thirty thousand years later, that changed. Somewhere in human history someone stopped, and instead of leaving their dead comrade lying in the ditch, they turned back, moved by the first flickering of grief and self-awareness. They turned back and initiated a most remarkable act – the first burial ritual in history. These first burial rituals were a response to the first 'heartbeat' of self-awareness – a sudden consciousness of one's own fate as a mortal being. This marked a fundamental change in human history. For the first time a human being had the first inklings that they existed – they were able to think, 'I exist'. Nothing else in creation was ever able to do this. And to be aware that you exist also means being aware that you will not exist – that you are vulnerable and will die. These are interdependent feelings. It was the sudden awareness of death that triggered human self-consciousness. Humankind had awoken from the sleep of unconsciousness to wakeful self-consciousness.

This first 'heartbeat' of self-awareness set in motion a chain reaction that woke humanity from its unconscious dream. Resounding like a drumbeat across the ages, it would change everything for ever. It is one thing to exist, but it is something else entirely to know that you exist. In all of nature, this know-ledge was like a laser beam piercing the dark universe. Humans had taken their first bite from the apple of self-awareness.

Early Archaeological Evidence of Ritual Activity

When early people first began to create a ritual of burying their dead they started to do things for reasons other than mere survival. This inclination blossomed into something quite extraordinary, as we shall see. The earliest evidence of this comes from Neanderthal people, about 100,000 BC. This activity is called ritual because it symbolises something else, something so much more than what it is. The evidence of our earliest ritual activity is associated with burial, which shows that the consciousness of death had kickstarted our awakening as a species. The issues that death raised for people were, 'What happened this person? She was walking around, warm and caring for the children and now she is as cold as stone. What happened her when she died? Where did she go?' This reflective searching was the start of our first religious, ritual and imaginative response to life.

If you remember what you were like when you were about four or five years old, you can get a feel for what early Neanderthal people felt. At that age you too were partly in a dream-like state and experiencing the first flickering of consciousness. This dream-like innocent state of childhood is sometimes broken by tragedy or trauma and, like death for early humans, accelerates the awakening of the human mind to mortality.

The other evidence of symbolic awakening is from early humans in Spain and France, who, some 42,000 years ago, created the first pieces of cave art. This early art illustrated figures of the gods and tried to reconcile life with death – just as we do today.

What we begin to realise is that, as early humans became increasingly conscious of their mortality, it awakened in them both dread and awe. As well as a real sense of dread about death, people also had a sense of awe and wonder in the face of the majesty of life.

Terror and Wonder

To be alive and to know that at some point you will die creates fear and terror. Just as you know the wonderful feeling of being alive, you are also disquieted by your own vulnerability and mortality. So, although you can achieve great things and have a rich and abundant life, at the same time you are trapped in a decaying body that goes the way of all living things. If that were not bad enough, you are also aware that death can strike at any time for reasons beyond your control. As any protective parent knows only too well, the risk of death lurks around every corner. These ideas have been articulated well by Ernest Becker and Sheldon Solomon.

We see in the artwork and rituals of ancient cultures that humanity also developed a sense of wonder at the majesty of Creation. Celtic people and their predecessors in Ireland, before the arrival of Christianity, for example, had a rich spirituality and a sense of the sacred in all natural life. All ancient cultures developed religions, beliefs and rituals that gave expression to this awe.

One does not need to go back in history to feel these things. There is something wonderful about being alive and just savouring your existence; it is probably the most sublime experience we know. Every once in a while, you will experience the exhilaration of being able to appreciate it. You think to yourself, 'It's great to be alive.' Other animals do not have this privilege. So the first heartbeat of self-consciousness awakened both wonder and dread not known to any other living organism.

For ancient people, this first heartbeat of self-consciousness was prompted by necessity, born of the proximity of death. Death was and is the one brutal fact of life that confronted people with their powerlessness and ultimate impotence. Death was the one constant that awoke humankind to its predicament. How humanity then dealt with death revealed everything we need to know about the emerging human psyche, as has been brilliantly articulated by psychologist Sheldon Solomon and anthropologist Ernest Becker.

It is for these reasons that discoveries about the burial rituals of ancient peoples are so fascinating – they reveal so much about the human condition and what really concerns us. Such discoveries also show that early humans displayed not just terror but a sense of the sacred, the sense of being a small part of a much bigger reality.

> The ancient stone monuments of Ireland are wonderful, weather-beaten witnesses to history. They have an ancient wildness that fits perfectly with the magical meanings that have been ascribed to them. There are about 1,500 megalithic tombs still evident in Ireland – all built between about 4000 BC and 2000 BC. Megalithic tombs like Newgrange in County Meath, which dates back to about 3000 BC, testify to the presence of an indigenous pre-Celtic culture that had clearly awoken to the human predicament. These megalithic monuments are a dramatic revelation of the religious and existential consciousness of the early Irish settlers. These people did not just exist; they were aware of the vulnerability and privilege of that existence and aware of the gods that made such existence possible — gods associated with the seasons, stars, animals, harvests and crops; the same things we depend on today but take for granted.
>
> Most of the megalithic monuments were tombs of some sort, and they reveal the religious and existential disposition of humankind. Rituals and religious ceremonies

were symbolic of people's relationship with their condition. Places of ritual show how the early Irish dealt with life and death and what the awakening meant. To stand in the middle of the stone circle of Drombeg in West Cork is to sense this awakening, to experience the meaning that is wrestled from the cosmos. To know that 'I exist', and that all about me things and people die, is a fearsome reality that lies at the heart of human existence.

Death and Desire

The emergence of self-awareness – the realisation that 'I exist' – was driven, therefore, by our psychological and physical confrontation with death. Of all the things our early ancestors had to deal with, the ever-present proximity of death was the primary one. This is self-evident given that the whole purpose of life, evolution and any creature's existence is to avoid death for as long as possible. This terror of death is at the heart of life itself. All living creatures, from ants to antelope, pulsate with the determination to survive and endure. It is what defines us and makes us what we are.

So for early people death was not an intellectual puzzle to be debated around the fire, but a relentless presence that saw the weak die off quickly. Let there be no illusions about the intensity of the will to survive in the face of death. Today we still experience this raw emotion when we get a fright or when an insect crawls across our skin. These are echoes of what life was like back then, but they are also indications of what lies at the base of our psyche and is repressed in the comforts of modern life.

This awakening to the fact that we exist, die and are dependent creatures is illustrated in the Celtic ritual celebrations of the seasons. The Celtic rituals were times when there was an open door between the real world and the otherworld, particularly at the winter and summer solstices, when the earth would turn towards or away from the sun, reminding people of their dependence on the gods of fertility, the land and the deities that looked after them.

The driving force of every living thing was (and is) to escape death, but, more important, to pursue more life. It is this desire to keep on going that defines life itself. If we did not want more life we would just lock ourselves in our houses and never come out. So escaping death is not all we live for. We have desire too! Just as a tiny seed grows and pushes itself up through soil towards the light, we humans also have this inner drive and determination to endure. The entire history of both animal and plant life on Earth shows this. As I shall show later in the book, this is what is heroic, not just in humanity, but in nature itself.

We wake up every morning ready to begin a new day and to endure and continue, with a naive physical optimism. We put aside our terror of death and live in accordance with an interior myth about our permanence; we get through our day feeling that we are as solid as stone. Yet, side by side with this optimism is a constant vigilance: every minute of every day we engage in subconscious activities aimed at defeating death, whether simply driving carefully or taking care as we cross the street. We persist as if we are immortal yet we live our lives knowing we are not. It is as true today as it was on the plains and dark forests familiar to early humans.

'Vertical' Awareness in a 'Horizontal' Life

You go through much of your day in a haze of automatic, stimulus–response activity at work, or just tick-boxing your way through your list of things to do. However, at certain moments you awaken to your own existence and feel the acute heartbeat of self-consciousness. It may be sitting alone in a café over a cappuccino; thinking about someone with affection; worrying about an illness; or feeling unexpected gratitude for something. These moments, these little shocks of awareness and appreciation of life, reveal your anxiety about how fragile life really is. The awareness of your vulnerability 'puts things into perspective'. It is something you try to keep to the forefront of your awareness to remain 'awake'.

Fionn Mac Cumhaill

The motif of an awakening is common in Irish mythology. Metaphors of discovery and transformation are central to most myths and legends. The well-known story of Fionn Mac Cumhaill tells the story of the hero-child being taken away from his parents in order to be safe from those who might want him killed and to learn the ways of the hero who would later be king. Hiding away under a false name, he learned the ways of life, the skills of the warrior and the intuitions of poetry. One day, while studying poetry under his mentor, he burnt his thumb while cooking what was called the Salmon of Knowledge. When he placed his thumb in his mouth and tasted the salmon he was awakened, after which he was transformed. Through self-knowledge, he suddenly became aware of his place in the world. Very interestingly, the old poet, who knew who he was, then asked him the key question. He asked him who he was. Fionn then declared himself by his full name for the first time. At that point the old sage knew that he could teach him nothing more. Fionn was awakened. He realised who he was and he followed his destiny towards greatness as a king. This might seem like a quaint old story, but embedded in it is the truth about awakening: that when you wake up to your real identity your destiny is revealed to you and you know what it is you must do.

A Psychological State of Emergency

Before self-consciousness and self-awareness, the human was like any other advanced animal. Animals just existed, following their instincts to survive. When humanity awoke, however, things began to change and the species began to develop in dramatic ways.

Now that humanity was fully conscious of death, a state of emergency was triggered; humanity felt the need to do something about its mortal predicament. And it did so. The first heartbeat of awareness – the 'I know that I exist' – was the awakening of humanity and what started as a flickering and a barely noticeable beat grew to become the pulse of all art, religion, literature and mythology. It became the soul of humanity. It was the wick from which the flame of psychological and spiritual life caught fire.

So the first awakening triggered awe and dread, gratitude and fear, love and terror. But before we move ahead we shall look at another significant and immediate consequence of this awakening: the blossoming of imagination.

The First Heartbeat of Imagination

As humans became aware of mortality, the flowering of the imagination was also triggered. How so? The only way you can think of your non-existence or death is to *imagine* it. Very simply, imagination is the ability to conceive of things that do not exist. Before all this, humans were like all other animals, accepting reality exactly as it was, without imagining an alternative. We humans are forever imagining alternatives to the reality we have been given. Even as you sit reading this book, in the back of your mind you are imagining other possibilities – if I do something, maybe things can be different. This thought is a simple exercise of imagination.

With imagination people began to consider their lives and predicament. All sorts of thoughts began to flow from that first rupture in the soil of human consciousness. Therefore, when Stone Age men and women stood at the crest of a hill, looking down into a fertile valley, they began to imagine the many possibilities and were filled with joy at what they could now imagine and make real. Another animal that reached the same point on the hill would never have any sense of appreciation or awe. For this reason humans can sit and glory in the beauty of a sunrise while a rabbit silhouetted against the same sun sees nothing.

This new imagination triggered an urge in humanity to express its awareness and awakening. In its at times excruciating self-consciousness, humankind was impelled to express what it now imagined and felt. This of course emerged in ancient art and rituals.

Newgrange

Every 21 December, at the winter solstice, when winter has reached its lowest point, the inner chamber of the ancient megalithic tomb of Newgrange, on the Hill of Tara in County Meath, is lit up by the rising sun. After the solstice the sun begins to rise earlier each day and light gradually returns to the land. Newgrange's passage tomb, built by Neolithic people some five thousand years ago, is an extraordinary monument both to imagination and to humanity's need to express wonder, gratitude, awe, terror and dependency in a life-affirming way. On the same day, at the Drombeg stone circle not far from where I live, the same setting sun is aligned with the two axial stones of the stone circle. Both of these celestial events, marked by our ancient ancestors, were an awakening to awe and dread, gratitude and respect, humility and courage. Human imagination enabled people to remember their past and imagine their future in a way that was inconceivable before. While the dread that is stirred by being aware of our predicament triggers all the ills that befall us psychologically, such as anxiety and depression, it is also countered by the gratitude, awe and a sense of the sacred stirred by the same heartbeat of awareness.

The awakening was the dawn of the human imagination, a capacity that when coupled with intelligence allowed us to plan ahead – to store provisions, develop better clothing and understand the seasons. Our developing capacity for foresight allowed us to imagine not just the future but also the threats that might compromise that future. So although we survived, we became anxious and preoccupied with safety from predators and illness. We also learned to 'time travel' in the mind, to see far ahead and to prepare for the future, or to recall the past and learn from it. We became as concerned about the 'there and then' as the 'here and now'.

So the dawn of self-consciousness was the dawn of imagination. Like a whale breaking the surface of the sea and glimpsing life above, humankind broke the surface of consciousness and saw possibilities for the first time. Humanity would now be able to do so much more than just exist in reality. It could do something about it. It could rise above it.

The Possibilities Created by Imagination

After the awakening of imagination came a flood of possibilities. Humanity was able to do more than just accept reality as it was – it was able to imagine it being different. Not only that, it could *make* reality different. Brilliant! All sorts of things began to appear. For example, when the nomadic tribe came to a narrow raging river, they would often turn back in search of another crossing point. Yet someone, at some point, imagined something that did not exist in the real world – a bridge! Thoughts could be made real, the world could be changed and people could adapt to make reality work. *Homo sapiens* had learned to adapt to all sorts of climates and landscapes by using imagination. To create a protective piece of clothing, one must first be able to imagine it. Necessity is the father of imagination, imagination the mother of invention and invention the child of intelligence.

At times in evolution there comes a jump, a quantum leap, as a species discovers more efficient ways to adapt and survive. For humankind, self-consciousness and the development of imagination was a dramatic leap that changed everything.

The Child's First Heartbeat of Imagination

If you think back to your childhood you can recall the trace elements of exactly what early humanity felt. Just recall those times when, as a child, you lay on your bed at night turning over the hopes, fears and dreams that flowed through your mind. You did not need to leave your bedroom to inhabit a rich, scary or wonderful world. Your imagination made all sorts of fears and hopes accessible to you, from the smaller fears evoked by bad dreams to larger domestic worries about abandonment, serious illness or a family death. More importantly, you will also have imagined fantasies of greatness, as a footballer, actress, dancer, celebrity, or some hero or heroine who would receive the acclaim of others. From the theatre of your imagination, as a child you were replicating the experience of ancient people, trying to comprehend the unknown, trying to cope with your actuality and destiny. This dawning of your own imagination from your unconscious existence as an infant was similar to what blossomed for humanity during its prehistory.

The First Religious Reflex

With the blossoming of imagination and the awareness of our place in the world came the dawn of religious feeling. This feeling was a response to the great unknowns that humanity encountered. Having awoken from the sleep of unconsciousness, humanity needed to respond to its mysterious existence and predicament. As a natural consequence, ancient nomadic tribes began to create simple rituals that brought order to the chaos and gave expression to what they felt.

They attempted to do this through the most elemental forms of simple things – art, music, rituals. All of this grew slowly into culture and religion. Humanity began to honour and worship the source and fragility of human life. It is interesting that some anthropologists are now suggesting that when early nomads gathered in groups, it was not only as a means of production and efficiency in getting food. It also served a religious function: in the midst of a chaotic and dangerous world, people gathered to pray in the archaic sense of that word – to console and bear witness. If you think of it, this makes sense. Even today, at times of tragedy or devastation, people will gather in small groups in order to engage in some sort of meaning-making and have their own distress shared and witnessed. This need is religious in the purest meaning of the word. The religious reflex is a topic we shall return to throughout this book, not as evidence of the objective truth of religion but as evidence of people's need to live by myths that inspire and sustain them.

The Awakening of Ireland

Much has been written about the awakening in Ireland, which occurred around the fifth century, and the rise of monasticism. The arrival of Christianity with St Patrick and a host of monastic missionaries triggered a gradual and ultimately dramatic awakening of the Irish as an astonishing monastic movement spread like wildfire through Ireland and, subsequently, Europe.

Monasticism took root in Ireland like nowhere else in the world. In a people who were already innately religious and who had a deep respect for the deities, it ignited the Irish soul in an extraordinary manner. Ireland took to monasticism as though it had been waiting for it for centuries. Bringing a focus, purpose and a means of elevation to a people who had been devastated by the plague and a natural disaster around AD 550, Christianity took root in Ireland without wars, martyrdom or conflict. The psychology of this remarkable period is fascinating; people's existential need for a ritual, symbolic and real way to have purchase and purpose in life was dramatic. The vertical (spiritual) life was reignited by monasticism, and the Irish discovered mindfulness nearly two thousand years ago. The hunger for a prayerful, peaceful, poetic and simple life was extraordinary. From this movement arose a host of heroes and saints who embodied the spirit of the awakening.

Something happens to your soul when you stand at the edge of Dun Aengus on the Aran Islands, one of the most magnificent ancient monuments to be found anywhere in Western Europe; when you climb to the top of Skellig Michael, one of the great wonders of the world, and marvel at the little stone huts of those early monks; when you stand at the centre of the stone circle at Drombeg in County Cork and imagine yourself aligned with the stars; when you hear the uilleann pipes play Cú Chulainn's lament at the beginning of *Riverdance*; when you crouch along the inner passageway of Newgrange imagining our Neolithic ancestors glorying in the rising sun; or when you read of the death of Cú Chulainn as he strapped himself to a standing stone so that he could meet death standing up. Your soul is awakened as you discover something that lies dormant within you. You awaken an eternal truth about your place in this world.

The awakening is the discovery that you do not live in reality; you live above and beyond it. This is, in fact, what evolution demands; it is the realisation of why hope is necessary. The awakening is the acknowledgement of the conditions of life and a response that is necessarily transcendent; it is the realisation that we must, by necessity, live an enchanted life; it is the existential shock of both delight and dread when we are fully awake to our fragile existence; it is a confrontation with complacency; it is realising that life is enchanted by the heroic and courageous impulse of humanity; it is the realisation that life requires something magical because human resources are meagre when set against the forces of life and death; it is realising why hope and inspiration are necessary and why imagination forces us to the cliff-edge to fly.

Chapter 3

The Taboo against the Truth

An Ancient Celtic Prayer
The sacred three
To save, to shield, to surround
The hearth, the house, the household,
This eve, this night.
Oh, this eve, this night,
And every night,
Each single night.

                                Carmina Gadelica (Vol. 1, 235)

To understand the meaning of ancient Celtic prayers one must understand the fear that inspired them. Most prayers of Celtic spirituality were written as cries for protection and safety – invocations that helped people face adversity with a feeling that the gods would care for them. However, the reason they were necessary is often neglected. People then lived in constant fear: life was harsh and they had none of the kind of medicines we now take for granted. Without the threat of life's real brutality, they would have had little need to seek

27

protection from the gods through prayer. Today, while we feel more secure, we are still as mortal as ever. We might live a bit longer, but the human body and psyche are unconsciously preoccupied with the same terrors. When we are able to accept the harsh truths about life, our understanding about why we do what we do is illuminated.

Another typical Celtic prayer reads:

> Be thou a bright flame before me,
> Be thou a guiding star above me,
> Be thou a smooth path below me,
> And be a kindly shepherd behind me,
> Today, tonight and forever.
>
> *Carmina Gadelica* (Vol. 1, 49)

Most of the prayers of Celtic spirituality are like this; they implore the 'gods' to shield, protect and guide. Embedded in them is the faith that protection and safety will be given by the god on whom the supplicant depended and who determined their fate. In this way, prayers quietened the fear that made them necessary.

This human fear is still present and very real for humanity today. At its root is the core truth about our existence: that at some point we will all die and there is nothing we can do to stop it. And yet, despite the presence everywhere of this fear, most of the time we avoid acknowledging or discussing it. Why is this?

The Taboo against the Truth

Acknowledging the truth about the human predicament is generally taboo in popular psychology. This is because it requires us to admit to some unpalatable realities about life that seem to fly in the face of positive psychology, optimism and the belief that we can 'make our dreams come true'. We recoil from any truth that suggests that we are not in control and are instead drawn to those that peddle a promise of an almost miraculous cure for depression, anxiety and stress. We do not really want to look at what it is that bothers us so much.

The thing is, we do not want to deal with the truth – we would prefer false promises, easy solutions and an approach that does not ask too much of us. We want techniques that will make us feel better without having to look at why it is that we need to feel better in the first place. We want the 'key' to success, or the 'secret' to happiness, or the 'steps' to freedom that allow us easy access to these things without having to name and face the demons that stand in our way. In fact, these common metaphors of 'keys', 'gates', 'steps', 'guarantees' and 'secrets' illustrate our desire for a stress-free emancipation from life itself. However, any approach to well-being that is built around a denial of essential truths will ultimately fail.

It is critical not to offer a prescription for the hopeful or enchanted life without having the courage to look directly at the terror and vulnerability that lie at the core of our being. We must embrace the hopelessness inherent in the human condition. We must not tolerate any false positivity that is motivated by a fear of dealing with the suffering and tragedy that attend human existence. While I will open the gate to human transcendence, I am obliged, first, to dwell on the need for such relief from the ordeal of life.

While this book does promise an awakening that allows the soul to fly, its starting point is the solid ground of intellectual and moral honesty. So I need to ask you to bear with the contents of this chapter. In being able to confront our existential taboos and admit to our essential fears we awaken to what is really going on. Thereafter we will experience a freedom that will illuminate life in a dramatic way. We must go down before we can rise up, we must walk through a valley of darkness on the way to the light. I promise you that what will be revealed will ultimately be inspiring and hope-filled.

We must be courageous enough to see why we want to feel better about ourselves in the first place. That means looking at what is permanently unsettled in our mind and heart. So, let's go. Though these early stages in our climb are steep, the vista that will open up later will be worth the effort.

The Five Existential Truths

1. You are not in control of your destiny

You are not in control of your ultimate destiny nor of your more proximate fate. When any philosopher or theologian reflects deeply about the human condition they eventually arrive at the realisation that despite all our worldly displays of competence, success and progress – both personally and socially – ultimately we are utterly helpless to overcome our condition and fate: that we will all die eventually and there is nothing we can do about it.

Everything we do exists under the shadow of this awesome truth. No matter how self-important we become, ultimately we all share the same destiny. What becomes startlingly apparent is that every person is striving to build an immortal scaffolding around a life that is destined to fall. There is nothing you can do to alter this uncomplicated destiny of ageing, decay and death. No matter what you do, achieve, proclaim or believe, your destiny remains unchanged. This truth underpins and explains everything about human behaviour and why we act as we do. There is hardly a myth, mythology or religion that does not have this truth embedded symbolically at its heart.

Hardly a week goes by that we do not hear some tragic news about someone we know. We are upset when we hear that a friend's parent has died, a neighbour has been diagnosed with terminal cancer, an old school pal has been in an accident, or a family member has had a breakdown. We are reminded every day that tragedy and fate can strike anyone at any time.

The American Romantic poet James Lowell, writing about the death of his beloved child in his powerful poem 'After the Burial', reveals how death and loss force anyone to lay down their arguments about a just or rational world:

> That little shoe in the corner,
> So worn and wrinkled and brown,
> With its emptiness confutes you
> And argues your wisdom down.

Such occasions of loss or tragedy stop psychologists, philosophers, theologians and scientists in their tracks. They can offer little consolation. Rational approaches to life are never sufficient because they cannot help us come to terms with either the terror or tragedy or with their consequences for us.

A great deal of the popular psychology alluded to above peddles the myth of achieving your personal destiny in life, yet it does so without revealing that the reason this appeals to you is because, behind it all, you have no control over your final destiny. You want to believe that your dreams can come true while at the same time turning away from the fact that the ultimate dream (to endure happily) does not. You cannot escape the tragic helplessness that attends all of life. We thrive on our small successes because, in the greater scheme, we face an ultimate failure. This sounds harsh, I know, but do not give up on me yet or try to argue this away. Life is painful in so many ways, but with the courage to accept these things we shall discover, too, the heroic nobility and potential of the human person.

This has to be the cornerstone of our understanding of what life is about. We cannot resolve or escape this basic reality, no matter how hard we try. The taboo against acknowledging the implications of death, psychological impotence and mortality is more powerful than taboos about sex, money or anything else. No matter how well and happy you are in life, the unwelcome guest of your own mortality is always there, sitting at the top table and putting everything in context, always threatening to spoil the party of your illusions.

Deep in our unconscious mind we are driven, then, by the fear of death. Even the innocent child shares this vulnerability and dread. Fears of monsters under the bed, bad dreams, nightmares, the terror of abandonment by parents – all these illustrate how the fear of death is subconsciously ever present in the vulnerability of the child and adult. It is indeed fascinating to observe the reaction of small children when they are bleeding after an accident or fall. 'I'm bleeding', a little child will wail after noticing blood streaming from their knee. The reaction reveals what a child intuitively knows about its own mortal vulnerability.

For this reason, and given the harsh realities of life, the stories and sagas of Irish mythology are not romantic fairy tales offering false optimism; rather, they are often passionate and brutal tales in which death is a constant presence. The myths and legends of ancient Ireland, such as the *Táin Bó Cúailnge*, reveal how heroes and heroines were defined by their attitudes to death. The ultimate hero was always the one who faced his own death with courage and honour – the hallmarks of the Celtic warrior – while ancient dramatic epics, such as Cú Chulainn, are often graphic stories of heroic battles. They expose the raw nerve of humankind's proximity to death. Bloody and sometimes grim, they nonetheless resonate because every day you face death's descendants in its many different forms. Fear of rejection, for example, is death's first cousin and a reminder of the feeling of mortality and vulnerability. If someone rejects you, you die a little and it awakens your worst fears. As we shall see, however, these fears are not fatal and can be transfigured.

What does it mean to accept the implications of this profound and unyielding truth? It means to know that one is destined to return to dust – to be food for the earth. It is to have emerged from nothingness, to live a passionate and earnest life, to achieve some sense of importance and meaning, yet with your destiny ultimately being to simply decay and die. Like a door slammed in the face of optimism or innocence, it feels desperately unjust not just to your mind, but to your body, which will fight and rail against it to your dying breath. The realisation that you are just a transient human seems to rub your face in the mud and push you further away from the possibility of some form of salvation or transcendence. 'Don't be morbid', I hear you cry, 'Too much truth is hard to bear.' It is, yes, but this book is about ways of making the truth not just bearable but a force for good in our lives and for living freely.

The painful truth causes many people to reject the idea of God. What kind of deity would allow suffering, tragedy, annihilation and genocides to befall innocent people on Earth? And yet, as we shall see, nestled in this crown of thorns there are jewels to be found, but before we talk about those, there are a few more thorns to be felt first.

2. You are not in control of your immediate fate

The truth is that you are not in control of life. However, most of us spend all of our time trying to control our life, our day, the people around us and the things we do. In fact, you might conclude that being in control is your main goal in life. And this is true in many senses.

In the first truth above I highlighted that you have no control over your fate. So many of our ancient myths tell us the same thing. You are not really the master of your ultimate fate. As if to remind us of this, the Irish legend of the Children of Lir tells the tragic tale of how the four daughters of King Lir were turned into four swans by their jealous stepmother and were destined to remain so for nine hundred years. King Lir spent the rest of his life visiting the lake and talking to his children. The story is painfully tragic and tells us simply that good does not always prevail and that we may have little control over how destiny shall befall us.

You know only too well that accidents, tragedies and illnesses can occur at any time and that fate seals your destiny without any consultation with you. You tend to be more aware of how those you love are vulnerable to such fate than yourself. So you worry greatly about the safety and well-being of your children, family members and parents, often in denial of the fact that fate will lay its hand on your own shoulder just as easily. You feel sorry for others who experience tragedy but are caught off guard when fate casts its shadow over your own family. So all your daily efforts to be well, secure and safe stem from the fact that deep down you are not in control. Simply put, you are not driving the bus of your own life. Regardless of all your status, success, achievements, how much you are loved, or how great you are, you are doomed to meet your destiny at a time and place and in a way that is not under your control. These are the simple and uncomplicated truths about being a mortal human being.

3. You are insignificant and therefore you strive for significance

Your urge to 'be someone' arises from your natural feeling of inadequacy in the face of everything discussed above. The reason we need to be significant – to feel we are people of value, to have self-esteem, to strive for more life – is very simply because of the underlying terror and insignificance that animate all of life. The universal urge to count in some way, however small, is rooted in our subconscious awareness of our existential insignificance.

This need to matter was awakened in humanity when we became self-conscious. The thing that motivates most human behaviour is not just to survive, but also to matter. By being 'somebody', we feel as if we have transcended the anonymity of mortality and the nothingness that it threatens.

As I have emphasised, we are not made merely to survive like an animal. We need to go out and find ways to feel good about ourselves by either joining with a larger purpose or else by doing the opposite – by standing out as an individual.

We can achieve significance in negative ways, including by abusing others – through domestic tyranny and abuse, aggression and violence; power and control; arrogance and narcissism.

However, we can experience our significance in much more benign ways, too, such as our little daily successes – those moments when we succeed in achieving some small goal, when we celebrate something, or when we receive some minor praise or accolade. The human need for recognition and praise reveals the uncertainty that lies beneath.

Most of us find a sense of importance in safe ways: we devote ourselves to bosses, leaders, partners, celebrities, teams or political parties. We accommodate and seek social approval and try to be a good provider, parent, employee or citizen. In this way we overcome the insignificance threatened by mortality, if only in little ways. There is nothing false about this. However, it represents both the truth and tragedy of our condition: We achieve our freedom within the four walls of what society provides. It is freedom, yes, but within certain constraints.

4. You have problems because you are trying to be other than what you are

With friends or family, a great deal of our conversation is about our relative success in dealing with obstacles and difficulties. If you think of your last conversation today, the chances are it was exactly like this. The problems may have been minor – like how you parked the car in a difficult space – but you can be sure the conversation was about overcoming some little adversity. This is a fundamental issue I'd like to reflect on. Why do we have problems at all and why do we always think about them? Why are we troubled like this and therefore so unlike most other creatures on Earth?

Right now, as you read this book, there is a reason you have problems to be solved, are anxious and unsettled, or feel inadequate in some way. That reason is fascinating and if you let it, it can be a light bulb moment, awakening you to so many other things: You have problems and find life difficult because *you are trying to be other than what you are.*

Beneath the surface, you are struggling against yourself. Because you are both a body-centred animal subject to fate *and* a psychologically centred human who strives to overcome this, you want more control and certainty than are available. Problems arise because while you are subject to fate and helplessness, you never cease trying to overcome them, or making an effort to be more than what you seem to be. You don't give up and you keep trying. And the reason such effort is needed is because of your willingness to try to overcome the limits of your own body.

Take any everyday problem you have. Dig deep enough and you realise that your problem is that you are trying to control something over which you have only some control. You are trapped in a body that defies your will and that aches, defecates, bleeds, decays and dies with you trapped in it. You are striving always to live, to survive, to overcome what life throws at you and to endure. The truth is that you are an imaginative, psychological being trapped in the body of a dying and decaying creature.

This is the problem and the root of all your little problems. It means that you are forever trying to be more than you are. You are always striving for more – more control, health, success, wealth and security. The reason you are striving is because you can never quite get enough of it. You want power, control and freedom but your body is rooted to the ground and keeps you trapped and somewhat impotent.

5. You have problems because you are an imaginative being dependent on a mortal body

You are both animal and angel, a poetic human trapped in a biological body. You search for control, significance, status, security and a promise that will give you a foothold in a life that slips away from you. You want to be the master of your own life, but your mortal body and its inadequacies defy you. You strive against yourself and it is both your blessing and your burden. You want to achieve things and be a success because deep down you want to defeat the helplessness that your mortal body causes you to feel. This, suggests Ernest Becker, is the conflict that lies at the core of our being.

You can contemplate the splendid universe and yet you reside in a flesh-covered skeleton – a body that itself is pumping blood to stay alive, driven by a life-battery that is being slowly drained of its power. You tell yourself that if only you were an animal (like a sheep) or an angel (like a god), you would have no fears, worries or guilt, or the desire to be different from what you are. As a god or an animal you would be without dread. You are therefore forever trying to be more than just the creature that you are. It is only when you feel the full strain of this conflict that you realise what an impossible situation it is for you to be in. Well, almost impossible. It is a problem that we cannot eliminate, but it is one that we can resolve, as we shall see!

Echoes of this duality are seen in our ancient myths, in which many characters and heroes were both godly and human. The kings in Irish mythology were often both gods and men. In some traditions the tribal king was ritually married to the tribal goddess Medb. Tir na nÓg was where Oisín was both human and godly. The Tuatha Dé Danann were the ancient tribe of the gods who inhabited Ireland before the Celts. They were mythologised as a magical people. In the spiritualities, mythologies and rituals of times past is found a tension between the mortal and divine worlds world and a sense of humans walking the threshold between the two.

The conflict for both ancient and modern humans is that we are forever grasping for some purchase on life just as we slide from a world that cannot hold us. As defined by philosophers down the ages, this is our core dilemma. And this is not a mere philosophical or religious problem – it is one you face every day. How do you let go your efforts to control your life and relationships and accept the limits of your nature and how, then, can you continue to aspire to something greater for yourself?

I said at the beginning of this chapter that we must be fearless in naming the truth about our nature, and this is it: The core of your problems is that you do not want to be the helpless animal that you are. That's the rub. Every day you strive to overcome your condition, to prove yourself. You want to be in control – to be a god with a small 'g', master of your own little world. Yet no matter how hard you try, you cannot quite do it. Sure, you get a taste of it when everything goes right, which contributes to the illusion that you have overcome the body and its limitations.

However, this lasts only until the next time you fall over, you get bad news, or serious illness strikes someone you love. Yet you are constantly wanting to transcend your very nature, to escape the injustice of life, to be travelling in something other than a mortal body. You want to fly. Like an angel.

Are there myths that tell us this? Stories such as Deirdre of the Sorrows, Diarmuid and Gráinne, and the Táin walk this ridge between the mortal and the magical. At the ancient Celtic festivals of the seasons, like Imbolc, Samhain, Bealtaine and Lughnasa, communities gathered to celebrate the new seasons, open the tombs and portals to the gods and acknowledge their dependence on a life bigger than their tribal squabbles. The unawakened mind looks back on those rituals as pagan, ignorant and little more than superstition, but this attitude closes us off from the essential nature of life and reality and fails to see how people today still engage in ritual life, just in different, more heavily disguised forms. (Sport is one obvious example of tribal, celebratory and combative rituals enacting the dramatic tussle between life and death, victory and defeat.) The point is that you are not a god but a mortal and as such you cannot escape your mortal form. The mythology evokes in many ways the reality of mortal helplessness and the need to appease the gods. At seasonal Celtic celebrations in ancient times the entryways to tombs were laid open to allow the ancestral gods to be released into the world to aid their people. The Irish poet Patrick Kavanagh, in describing his love for a woman in 'On Raglan Road', also expresses his dilemma in terms of the human and the angelic: when he, an angel, did not allow that she was a mortal being he would 'lose his wings at the dawn of day'.

41

The Taboo

There is a universal taboo against acknowledging the truth of what is written in this section. You may want to reject it, fearing that it is too negative. But let's consider, then, what that negativity signifies.

Highlighting our mortal fallibility is taboo because it seems to take the wind out of our sails, leaving us feeling exposed. To name it is to be accused of being morbid, when in reality you are revealing a truth that few dare to admit, a truth that at times seems genuinely too much to bear, however simple its meaning. Socially and culturally, then, exposing our animal nature is taboo because it highlights the illusion by which we live as a society – that we must act as if we are special, if not immortal. If you have visited a hospital recently, you may have been taken aback by how much pain and suffering remain hidden from public view. The painful and degrading process of dying and death itself is something we prefer not to know about. The taboo against all of these kinds of things is pervasive.

Civilisation seems to demand that we conceal those behaviours that reveal our animal nature, be they sexual or emotional. Harmless animal behaviours such as farting, belching, scratching and drooling are all taboo precisely because they show our animal nature in action. We shrink from the tiniest signs of our mortality even as we strive to feel special and chosen.

The social taboo against talking about one's own death, or the death of someone one knows, is a very real example of this and generally considered to be appalling. To say to an elderly relation, 'I think you are going to die in the next few months' would be considered not just taboo, but unforgiveable. To tell an adult that no matter how fast he runs, death is still gaining on him feels like telling a child there is no Santa. To speak such truths aloud is to uncover the illusions, however essential they may be, on which our lives are based. The point I make is simple, but to realise the deeper meaning of these things is difficult. It is hard to see how our psychological denial of death runs to the very core of our being. It is also hard to see that the more strenuous the denial, the more invulnerable and in control we strive to be.

All of this is articulated brilliantly by anthropologist Ernest Becker when he says, in effect, that the denial of death is the denial of our animal nature. The denial of our animal nature is the denial of our mortality. The denial of mortality is the denial of vulnerability. The denial of vulnerability is the promotion of righteousness. The promotion of righteousness is the beginning of self-elevation. The elevation of the self is the diminishment of others. The diminishment of others is the beginning of the degradation of others. The degradation of others is abusive. And abuse of others perpetuates evil and begins with the denial of our mortal vulnerability.

The redemption of the world will be found in the heroism of those who inhabit human vulnerability and, through this, feel a compassion and sympathy for life.

All this does not mean, however, that you must confront this taboo and tear it down wherever you see it. No, you need only be aware of it, because although it is based on some denial, it is also, more importantly, based on a need to cultivate life-enhancing illusions that help us to overcome what life throws at us. (I use the word 'illusion' for now, but it is more than that, as we shall see.) So you would not dream of saying to your elderly relation that they are on 'borrowed time', or tell a person suffering from chronic illness to give up because it is pointless. To do so would be preposterous and sadistic. This is because we all live, survive and thrive on essential and necessary illusions.

The heroic urge in all of us cannot ever be quenched or fully named because it lies at the source of our will to endure. Our awakening to the fact that we exist and die triggered a stunning human response – the urge to transcendence.

The Celtic Cross symbolises a great deal of what I am trying to express. It is a simple unifying symbol for the human condition, the harsh truths of life and the transcendent invitation. The Celtic Cross symbolises how we exist in two dimensions – in a horizontal physical reality and in a vertical spiritual reality. Where the vertical and horizontal truths intersect at the centre is where the eternal intersects with the mortal, where the invisible meets the visible, where your need for control meets your need to let go. And it is to the deeper meaning of this symbol that we shall now turn.

Chapter 4

The Celtic Cross

All things are inconstant except the faith in the soul,
which changes all things and fills their inconstancy
with light.

James Joyce, letter to Augusta Gregory
(22 November 1902)

The Celtic Cross stands in the background of the Irish psyche. Whether at the crest of a hill, leaning in the long grass of an old graveyard, or protecting the stone walls of a monastery, it reminds us who we are. It awakens the feeling of memory and of the heroic elements of our history. One does not need to be a historian to be moved by the evocation of this ancient image. The Celtic Cross stirs the Irish soul and seems to embody the sufferings and stories of its people. More than a Christian image, it is a standing stone, a proud defiance, an ageing gladiator still facing down wave after wave of invaders. It seems at once to be every hero who stood against the elements that battered the ancient coast of Ireland. The Celtic Cross refuses to yield its honour to death or time. In so doing it stands wordlessly as a portal to the worlds of ancient Ireland. Across the misty graveyards of Ireland's villages, it leans into the gales of history. Hundreds of years later it still stands proud in the long grasses, its strength fading but unbowed, waiting for the gods to say, 'It's okay, your work is done.' Every stone cross leaning in a graveyard or at the brow of a hill stands for you, asking you to now help hold it up.

Its beauty is its brokenness, its irregular wildness, the lichen of old wounds that scar its surface, the winds of an open sky that blow through its eyes. In its steadfast and reliable silence, it refuses to give up its secrets for interrogation by modernity. For the eternal truths, there are no words, no confessions to be made, only the stand of being.

The Celtic Cross asks you who you are. Like an ancient druid, a forgotten ancestor, an unnamed saint, a monk, a poet, or a wounded God, it asks you to bear witness. It offers reassurance and stands as a breakwater of empathy against whatever adversity crashes upon your shore.

The Celtic Cross is aligned with all the other standing stones and stone circles of Ireland. In ways it precedes its Christian origins because it was created to honour ancient history, to mark the nature of the human condition and to mark a new beginning. In the stone itself, there is a measure of eternity that draws the heart back to the peoples who inhabited this land before history.

So as you walk the long grass of the graveyard, the river sweeping quietly by its walls, you stumble from tomb to tomb squinting at names erased by time, until you find

your own name there, buried among the forgotten. Here
your grandfather, there Fionn Mac Cumhaill and over here
Ferdia, who died at Cú Chulainn's reluctant hand, and
under the old tree you hear the faery voices of famine
children whispering in the shade. Everywhere the ghosts
of who you are swirl in mist and sky. The grief of
unwitnessed suffering and the joy of emancipation create
a music of their own, a dance across glens and rivers of
'the waters and the wild' flowing from the otherworld. The
Celtic Cross holds you up like the standing stone that
held Cú Chulainn as he died, determined to face his death
and enemies with courage – and standing up.

In the introduction to his book *The Redress of Poetry*, Seamus
Heaney references the two different and often contradictory
dimensions of reality within which we exist and urges us to
find a way of keeping a foot in both. Heaney indicated that
the crossing from the domain of the matter-of-fact into the
domain of the imagined was a central theme in his work. It is
also the central theme of this book: how to keep a foot in
both the mundane and the marvellous.

The image of the Celtic Cross captures the essence of this in
a symbolic way. It is a unifying symbol of our spiritual and
physical life. I will use it not as a Christian symbol, but as a
universal one. It is an archetypal image that symbolises both
the horizontal and the vertical dimensions of life – the kind
of unifying symbol that analytical psychologist Carl Jung
suggested we lose at our peril.

We will examine the three simple elements to the cross: the vertical axis, the horizontal axis and the circle in the centre, and show how this simple image encapsulates four simple but profound truths about life. That we have a vertical life; that we have a horizontal life; that both worlds meet within the circle; and that the 'burning point' of life is where they intersect.

Your Horizontal Life

The horizontal axis of the cross is symbolic of your literal life, your everyday life of automatic routine. Characterised by obligations and responsibilities and concerned with survival, it is devoted to trying to control life, master circumstances, get rid of obstacles and solve problems as they emerge. It is everything you do that is either automatic or determined by circumstances.

Your Horizontal Self is thinking all the time, making lists of things to do, pushing you to be productive. It is concerned with the four S's of status, safety, survival and significance. For these reasons, it is the self that becomes stressed, anxious and frustrated. Your Horizontal Self is preoccupied with these things and goes through life in the trance of getting from one day to the next. It has not awoken and instead drives forward, often worn down by stress and the compulsion to succeed.

Success on this axis is measured by such things as social status, financial security and self-importance. The self-esteem of the Horizontal Self rises and falls with this kind of success. At its best the Horizontal Self is going through the motions in a content way, secure in its own self-importance and committed to the concrete world of visible objects and obligations. At its worst it is driven by a need to control self and others in an agitated or anxious way, avoiding vulnerability, denying the existential facts of life and instead preferring to live in ignorance rather than enlightenment. Your Horizontal Self needs to be in control and does not want to be distracted from its compulsion to get what it needs. Oblivious to the human condition, it rarely lifts its head from what is close at hand to taste the air or to consider what lies beyond.

As we shall see, we get trapped in this world and in this self. Devoid of self-awareness and in denial of its human vulnerability, this self falls under the spell of horizontal preoccupations and can lose touch entirely with the vertical life. We live on the horizontal level most of the time, however, preoccupied as we are with the worries of everyday life and our attempts to secure our status, safety, survival and significance.

Your Vertical Life

The vertical axis represents the self that is not tied to the circumstances of life. It is the self that is awakened when the heart monitor of the soul 'blips' – when you are aware that you exist. It is your elevated self that might be considered spiritual or philosophical. It is your soul. It is the self that can rise above circumstances and horizontal preoccupations and experience life in a full and rounded way. To the degree that the Horizontal Self is narrow and constricted, the Vertical Self is open and expansive.

Not defined by circumstance, your Vertical Self was there when you were born. It was with you when you played as a child and as you grew up. It is therefore not tied to the present. Your Vertical Self remains untouched by stress and worry and is aligned with something far more permanent. It is awake to the narrative of life. Your Vertical Self experiences awe, gratitude, beauty, sorrow, delight and a connection with something above and beyond your horizontal worries.

The vertical axis can be imagined as rooted in the soil of one's soul and rising upwards to the liberation of one's spirit. 'Soul' refers to the deeper experiences of grief, loss and suffering. At the level of soul we are aware of our mortality and the earth from which we have emerged. 'Spirit' refers to all those transcendent experiences that enable us to rise above our horizontal condition and bring a lightness of heart, joy and hope. It is the light-heartedness and cheerfulness that comes from a gratitude for existence, for just being in the world.

Sorrow and joy are part of the Vertical Self because they are the twin emotions triggered by openness to mortal life itself. On this dimension we are attuned to the beauty and fragility of life. We see our horizontal stresses and worries for what they are – preoccupations and distractions from the essentials of life.

The Horizontal and Vertical Life in Celtic History

In Celtic mythology and spirituality there is a wonderful tension between horizontal reality and the vertical imagination. It is evident in most of the stories and sagas of what is called Ireland's Mythological Cycles. Virtually every tale or epic creates this tension within its narrative. These stories tell the listener that *things are never as they seem*. Even to this day, folklore suggests the same; all around you exist invisible presences.

In Deirdre of the Sorrows, the imagination and magic of Deirdre come into conflict with the horizontal reality of Conchubar. In the Children of Lir a magic spell dooms the children to a life trapped in the bodies of swans for nine hundred years. In almost every story, the magical vertical realm is central to the narrative and the transformation of the characters. The stories awaken the human heart to its predicaments and elevate the person into this vertical sensibility. This is essential to storytelling and is not merely a way of seeing the world: it is the way the world is. We like to think of this imagination and fantasy as a way of coping with horizontal reality when, as we shall see, it is a way of revealing vertical reality.

The Circle of your Life

The Celtic Cross is made complete by the circle, which draws together and integrates the vertical and horizontal axes. To live a full and meaningful life we must live on the two levels. If we are totally horizontal we are permanently anxious, stressed and driven to prove ourselves. If we are totally vertical we are zoned out and cut off from the ordinary everyday obligations of life. In other words, we cannot have our head in the clouds when everyday life insists we engage with it, but neither can we remain trapped in the obsessiveness of horizontal stressful living; we must be able to rise above it and remember what is essential in life.

The circle of the cross is a symbol of the integration of the two selves, of the two ways of being. Therefore, the cross becomes a symbol of human integration. When this happens, our vertical awareness imbues the ordinary activities of everyday life with extraordinary meaning.

As a symbol, the Celtic Cross asks that your life is lived within the circle, where your vertical life is grounded and your horizontal life elevated. To put it another way, your ordinary life must be open to its extraordinary existence; your imaginative life must be animated through your physical life. Your psychology or spirituality must be rooted in the ordinary and the everyday. And equally, your everyday horizontal obligations must have a vertical meaning if you are to be able to cope with them.

There is a legend that told of how St Patrick was shown a sacred standing stone marked with a circle that was symbolic of the moon goddess. The story goes that Patrick blessed the stone by making the mark of a cross through the image of the moon, making the first Celtic Cross. This legend implies that Patrick integrated the ideas of the ancient druids into Christian practices. This is more folklore than fact, but it is appealing in its image of integration. The moon, as a symbol of our mortal frailty and connection with natural creation, is the circle within which we stand, from where we see life in the round and where our vertical and horizontal lives converge.

At the centre of the Celtic cross
Of your own life,
There is a tree.
Lean against it.
Let go of searching and grasping for more.
Let the burning of your vertical life
Take root.
Stand.

The Burning Point of your Life

When we are living at our best we live close to the centre of the cross, exactly where our two selves are integrated into one. This is the burning point of life – where you live a passionate and full life. This is where you walk with an inner contentment, a feeling that what you do serves a higher purpose. There is a realisation that you are not defined by horizontal things – whether status, security or success. The centre burns when vertical passion ignites horizontal obligations. If you live within the circle, at the burning point, your day, your job, your illness, your worries are all elevated in a way that gives them an inner purpose and meaning that still makes life worth living. At the burning point you stay vertical, you remain awake with a deep awareness and you ascribe to ordinary suffering a purpose and promise that lie beyond it. We must live within the circle, at the burning point of life where our horizontal preoccupations intersect with our soulful and spiritual existence. At the burning point, ordinary life is lived in the context of an extraordinary existence.

In its efforts to awaken you to the essentials of life, there are times when your Vertical Self breaks into your Horizontal Self, through the simple emotions of sorrow or joy. When you are touched by grief it is as if a hand is placed on your shoulder that awakens you to what you have avoided. These are the experiences in life when suffering, loss or pain forces you to see life with a vertical eye. Grief, bereavement and the minor sorrows of life awaken you to the fragility, vulnerability and preciousness of life. This moment of awakening may be triggered by an illness that has befallen one of your children, the death of a parent, a health scare of your own, the loss of a job, or the emotional suffering of someone you love.

Adversity is often the only thing that makes us reassesses our identity, and that awakens us to our vertical life. Essential for growth and change, sorrowful or traumatic experiences cause you to remember who you are and who you could be. You remember the person you used to be and call him or her back. If you do not have a 'vertical' co-ordinate in your life you are trapped in the horizontal. You flee from the Celtic circle of your own life, slip further and further away from your real self and get caught up in the fabricated life.

At the burning point of life, we experience a gratitude for life; the sudden shock of being aware of what it is to exist at all; eternity breaking into and shaking up everyday life; a depth to our lives that comes of being present in all things; and the astonishment of the sacred. At this point, the enchanted reality is partly, though never fully, revealed.

Slaves to the Horizontal

When we become slaves to the meanings we draw from our horizontal lives, we then have to be sustained by them. These meanings are usually wealth or financial security, approval or acceptance, goal achievement or productivity. The horizontal life is, however, too one-dimensional and too dependent on external factors ever to be secure. If meaning in our lives comes from horizontal reality, our centre of gravity no longer resides within us and our self-esteem becomes a reflection of something or someone else.

If we see things too realistically we become turned in on ourselves. We lose touch with the sense of possibility and magic. And when we become too absorbed with the horizontal worries of everyday life, we come to believe that the resolution of these horizontal concerns will lead to peace and happiness. Then we are trapped as we seek a horizontal solution to a vertical life. The awakening is to see this. It is also to have a *feeling for* where you must look to for sustenance.

The Tear-point of your Life

The Celtic Cross as an image reveals what happens to us when we are emotionally moved and brought close to tears by joyful events. The tear is a unique and revealing sign of being human. In particular, tears that come when one is moved by significant and joyful events reveal something profound about human sensitivity and empathy. We let these things pass and often dismiss our tears as trivial sentiment. In doing so, we often fail to realise that they are in fact a profound revelation of an unexpected vertical meaning in an ordinary horizontal event. I call this the tear-point – those moments when you are deeply moved by the hidden truth of an ordinary situation. When these tears fill your eyes, it is a give-away, an everyday revelation of the existence of the vertical self.

This tear-point is often sentimentalised and dismissed, yet it reveals something quite profound about the human heart. Tears give the game away and expose your deeper nature. They are evoked at the burning point of life, when your everyday life intersects spontaneously with your spiritual life. You are momentarily aligned with your deepest nature and feel relief in being so. In these moments things fall into place and the true meaning of what is happening breaks through.

The Irish poet William Butler Yeats refers to human tears as the love-dew of mortality that dims our eyes. In *The Wanderings of Oisin* he wrote:

> But the love-dew dims our eyes till the day
> When God shall come from the Sea with a sigh
> And bid the stars drop down from the sky,
> And the moon like a pale rose wither away.

At the tear-point we sense the inevitability of these falling stars. I am not referring here to tears of sorrow or self-pity but to the tears of awakening that come when we are moved by a moment or occasion that reveals the vertical reality which until then had seemed hidden in the horizontal. The human tear, in this kind of instance, disarms the Horizontal Self, which is forced to give way to the vertical intuition. The tear is the Vertical Self that breaks through. It reveals your vulnerability and hope, woven into one sacred moment.

For example, you tear up when you watch your young daughter alone on stage at a school musical singing her little piece. The vertical breaks in on you and the real vulnerability of her life and your influence on it are revealed in what you think is a moment of weakness, but is in fact your revelation and redemption. At this moment, everything falls into place and you see into the life of things. Like a wave, your wordless awareness of your child's courage as she faces into a life of uncertainty and suffering passes over you in a brief moment.

You may be moved to tears by an unexpected empathy shown to you, or when you witness your child overcome some small adversity, or when you hear a song that awakens dormant grief, or when your local team wins some 'silly' game. At the tear-point, both joy and grief are present. The joy is the intense love and delight you experience in some exquisite moment, like watching your child head off to school. The grief is in knowing you will never be able to capture that love and that every beautiful thing in life passes. So, as you watch your little daughter leave your side and skip her way to school, tears come to your eyes as your love for her wells up and you realise that, despite this love, you can't protect her from all the sufferings of life that await her. Your heart breaks with such love, a love at the burning-point of life.

Tears of Awakening, not Sentimentality

Such tears are not tears of self-indulgence but of a joyful gratitude woven with an indescribable sorrow. They are moments that, as Heaney wrote, 'Catch the heart off guard and blow it open'. You are awakened to something that you often prefer to avoid, but when moved by it, you feel you are coming home to something in you that needs your recognition. The tear gives expression to what needs to be made visible. We experience these exquisite, touching, dramatic moments in many ways. For example, when someone you love experiences some victory in life after a great deal of effort – finishing a marathon or receiving an award. These moments are the stuff of life, because they reveal the 'effort' and fortitude asked by life. The tear is a wordless vertical revelation of the ordeal of life and of the quiet heroism needed to overcome it.

The Tear-point of Vulnerability

As I said, the tear-point gives the game away. Though most of the time you can keep your human vulnerability hidden, tears reveal the real truth – that your Vertical Self is attuned to the vulnerability and beauty of life that your Horizontal Self ignores. The tear-point reveals that under the arc of life all things are vulnerable in their beauty and transience. It is an ache that is at times too much to bear.

When you reach your tear-point you usually say, 'I'm just being silly' when in fact you are, possibly for the first time, being real. So, when you tear up at your daughter's wedding, or your husband's all-clear after a health scare, your vertical world intersects with the horizontal. This moment reveals your vertical awareness that, for example, what you have always done as a parent was helping others through a precarious life and you tear up when you see them get there safely. Your emotions break at these points because the ordinary moment, like a birthday, contains within it an extraordinary revelation about life itself.

Your Vertical Self does not have a voice; instead, it connects with the standing stones of your inner life and its landscape of dreams and imagination. The surfacing of tears is a breaking through rather than a breaking down: the shell of your Horizontal Self cracks and through the fracture, the soul begins to flow out in tears. Though it may feel as if 'I am falling apart', it is really a falling back together, a reintegration at the centre of the cross of your own life. The tear is wonderful. It is the water of life breaking through the crack in the porcelain self and revelling in the richness of the human struggle. Life is sorrowful and in many ways tragic. When you reach your tear-point, your body lets go a little, you stop trying and for a moment, your heart lifts, 'For the world's more full of weeping than you can understand' Yeats wrote.

The Celtic Cross

The seat of your soul is where your inner and outer worlds meet, where your vertical life intersects with your horizontal one. The Celtic Cross is therefore a harmonising symbol and it is the hope of the enchanted life to harmonise your horizontal life with your vertical one. So I invite you to:

> Lift your tired eyes from the urgency of the trivial
> And see the Celtic cross of your own life
> Set against the sky.

When you go vertical you see that the horizontal reality is a diminishment, a narrowing down of your life. It is a constriction of both who you are and who you might yet become. The ultimate reality is that we cling on to life in a body that has to let it go. When you have the courage to see this core reality, your vision is filled with compassion and a pathos that facilitates the transcendent response and allows you to rise to the occasion. You give hope, joy and good cheer a place of purchase in your life.

Part 2

The Enchanted Life

Chapter 5

A Celtic Introduction to the Enchanted Life

The heroic nature of Ireland's monastic awakening is a case study of the human enterprise. It reinforces the attitude to life emphasised in this book, an ancient en-*courage*-ment that arises from the suffering, bravery and ordinary inspiration of a people. Therefore my hope is that when you get a sense of the dramatic awakening that Ireland went through from the fifth to the twelfth centuries you might also hear it as a lyrical epic poem about your own life and understand that it opens the path to personal change. The tomb at Newgrange is a passageway to your own inner awakening; the Celtic Cross is an image of your own life; the death of Ferdia was your own psychological trauma; Cú Chulainn strapped to the standing stone at Clochafarmore in County Louth is you facing your own ordeals; the stone circles of ancient Ireland dare you to be steadfast in facing your immediate future. The saints and early monastics who spearheaded the monastic movement (such as St Columcille, St Columbanus, St Finian, St Enda and St Brendan) literally and symbolically represented your universal human urge for a transcendent, imaginative, heroic and spiritual life as a response to a harsh and sometimes unforgiving existence. They represent what much of Part 2 of this book encourages – a heroic and transcendent life.

Until its monastic awakening, Ireland had a mystical, 'mad' and magnificent history. Before the arrival of Christianity we were left to our own devices for hundreds of years. During all this time, as can be seen in our mythology, folklore and Celtic aesthetics, the Irish developed a spirituality and meditative disposition that was unseen elsewhere in the world. The mythological legends are filled with references to trans-cendence, the otherworld, enchantment, the gods and the ancestors from whom the Irish are descended. Scholars have noted the uplifting nature of Irish legends, myths and rituals, which apparently contrasts with the dark themes of Nordic or German myths. The Irish had developed a mystical light-heart-edness alongside the brutalities of life. The artistic embellishment of the gospels with colour, drawings and Celtic lettering, as in the Book of Kells, is just one example of the illumination of the Irish soul. Over hundreds of years, the Irish had developed an inner spirituality and a robust sense of who they were that allowed them to take the message of Christianity without bloodshed and to convert it into something extraordinary. It exploded with a vibrancy and honesty that few more institutionalised nations could have managed.

The Landscape of the Imagination

In metaphorical terms, Ireland's monastic awakening produced what might be called the provinces of the enchanted imagination. Part 2 of this book explores these provinces: to overcome through heroism; to illuminate through enchantment; to rise above through transcendence; to see into through poetry; to see beyond through imagination; to see beneath through myth; and to take off through Mind-Flight – the human mind's ability to create life-enhancing illusions that allow us to rise above our circumstances. These are the sparkling jewels in the crown of thorns we call life. In the following chapters we shall look at each of these magnificent human qualities as they have emerged in the face of an at times overwhelming life.

We see many of these characteristics in Celtic spirituality, monasticism, the mythological cycles, Celtic symbols and in the character of Irish saints like St Brendan or St Colmcille. These men, it should be noted, were saints not in the modern sense of the word, but assumed sainthood as a form of legendary recognition of their contribution to Ireland's psychological awakening.

This story of Celtic spirituality began with the extraordinary imagination of a people left undisturbed for hundreds of years to develop their own native mythology. This history is still relevant to you. The poet, the monastic, the urge towards the transcendent and immanent, is part of your own soul. It is marked in ancient monuments, sites and place names. It's the story of human inspiration and the desire of the human soul to 'fly.'

Strive to become the Champion of your Own Awakening

The stories of prehistoric Ireland and early Christian monasticism tell you that the anxiety and suffering you may be experiencing right now were known intimately by these ancient people. These tales suggest that your task in life is not to sink into the mud of disappointment and frustration, but to keep trying to rise above them and their deathly effects. It is the striving rather than the success that makes you human. Many of our wonderful ancient stories, folklore and legends encourage us to do exactly this. Think of it: what you love in someone is not how successful they are but their effort, not their victory but their courage. In this way, what you love in your spouse, partner or children is the way they face life's adversity, how they keep trying. This trait is what you will eulogise when they die – their hope and their courage.

You must bring the light of hope and your monastic intuition back into the darkened countryside of your own heart. You must take flight away from that which darkens your soul. You can find your own remote places, your rocky hermitage and your scriptorium to champion your own awakening. You must not remain entangled in trying to prove yourself to others. Perhaps you must choose the austerity of a 'holy' life inspired by simple need and uncomplicated virtue.

When St Finian set off in his currach to set up the monastic site on Skellig Michael he was a courageous hero who was making his transcendent urge physically real. He set off willing to face the harsh truths of life. He did so with imagination and a conviction in his ability to transcend suffering and with a lightness of heart that illuminated the pilgrimage of his life. When St Brendan, who founded the monasteries of Clonfert and Annaghdown, set sail from the Dingle peninsula he did so in search of the Beyond, a place that still waits to be discovered in your own inner world. When St Enda sought out the barren landscape of Inis Mór, which like the Skelligs stands against the rage of the Atlantic Ocean, he did so because of heroic imagination and the ability to live an enchanted life in the midst of abject hardship. When St Columbanus, the father of European monasticism, went on his heroic pilgrimage across Europe setting up monasteries of scholarship wherever he went, he was engaged in Mind-Flight, in rising to the occasion of life in an extraordinary way. He travelled through France, Switzerland and Italy to be the inspiration for St Francis of Assisi and left the monastery at Luxeil as a leading centre for a thousand years and the springboard for hundreds of monasteries in Europe.

It is all a magnificent and inspiring narrative about how we function at our best in the luminous world between the 'here and now' and the 'there and then'; how Mind-Flight is a metaphor for how we transcend the harsh circumstances of life; how who we are is also a spell we cast to enchant both others and ourselves; how we are at once mortal human and eternal angel; how the fronting up to the brutal truth of life awakens the religious reflex and the poetic imagination; how life demands a heroic response that is a form of transfiguration and transformation; how the awakening to one's human predicament fosters honest faith and is what the Danish philosopher Søren Kierkegaard called 'the spirituality of the shipwrecked'; how life is lived on both the vertical and horizontal dimensions; and, to the degree that we remain vertical, our Horizontal Life is aligned with our vulnerable nature and is thus redeemed.

The Universal Urge to Transcendence

In Chapter 3 I identified the truths that are taboo in life, but it is not enough merely to identify them; we must consider how we respond to them, because it is how we respond to the brutal truths of life, not how we avoid them, that makes us magnificent. And humanity has had to respond. Our ancestors *had* to respond to the tragedy, trauma and terror that followed them wherever they went. Today we do not just become passive depressed creatures because of these things. Not at all. We do so much more. While we deny and seek to escape death, denial only goes so far because reality catches up pretty quickly.

When denial failed and humanity stood squarely facing into the storm of life itself, it developed a quite extraordinary response. In many ways this book is about this response. The universal urge to transcend emerges from the harsh truths of life. Transcendence, enchantment, heroism and imagination have no meaning or purchase unless one sees the need for them. To ignore the brutal truths of life, to deny death, is to deny the necessity of the poetic and imaginative life. This is why vulnerability, when it is twinned with courage, is the most noble of dispositions.

Since the dawn of awareness, humanity has therefore developed a quite magnificent ability to rise above reality, to give it a meaning it never quite had, to see in reality what was not actually visible and, in this way, somehow to make it sacred. What enabled people down the ages to survive and thrive was not how they accepted reality as it is, but how, in effect, they refused to do so and instead partially transcended it with imagination, courage and life-affirming illusions.

The magnificent and marvellous quality in the human person is their ability to rise above the tragic in life. This psychological elevation and imagination is not an 'airy-fairy' form of spirituality but an essential and defining mythology. This ability to refuse to accept reality is so much more than just defiance or denial. It is a religious or spiritual response essential to the human enterprise, it is what inspires us and enables us to endure. It is the magnificent trait of the human being and our greatest resource.

In spiritual terms it is hope. In physical terms it is endurance. In psychological terms it is courage. In human terms it is transcendence. In child-like terms it is magic.

At its best it looks reality and truth in the face, accepts human vulnerability and the tragic in life, but goes beyond it. It rises above reality not so far as to be removed from it but far enough to transcend it. This and only this is what matters in the end. With their feet on the ground, the human person reaches for the stars.

Celtic spirituality is often romanticised and divorced from the extremely harsh living conditions of our early ancestors, conjuring up images of a people dancing along the boreens and byways of Ireland. Nothing could be further from the truth. Life was horrendously difficult. In fact the extraordinary fact that Christianity arrived in Ireland without any bloodshed or conflict is testimony to the need of a people to embrace a new promise of redemption or relief. It is a rarely quoted fact that before the monastic movement of early Christian Ireland and Celtic spirituality caught fire, Ireland experienced a major natural catastrophe: around AD 535 something happened that blotted out the sun for a couple of years all over Europe and further afield. It was also a time when the plague had reached Ireland from Europe, causing tens of thousands to die and breaking down the royal dynasties. Some have suggested that the mid-sixth century was the most important period in Irish history. Seeking some relief or promise, the people of Ireland were ready for something new and the monastic life took fire in a blaze that was to burn across Europe and bring light back into the Dark Ages of Europe. Like you, the Irish needed to find a way to transcend the conditions of life. As we have seen, the urge to do so is universal.

History is testimony to the urge to evolve, change and overcome – to keep on trying to transcend circumstances. Without this urge to transcend there would be no history because things would just stay more or less as they are. We would develop at a pace so glacial as to make change negligible from generation to generation. People would change no quicker than the mountains. But this is not the case. Humanity is driven by a passion to be more than it is. Even your own life is an illustration of this: you are reading this because something in you is searching for something more. You relate to the world and are not just absorbed into it. *That* you keep going is biological. But *how* you keep going is surely religious.

Chapter 6

An Ancient Irish Recipe for Life and Living: Seven Truths

In my desire to understand the universal urge to transcendence in the face of a difficult life, I was drawn away from psychology towards Irish mythology. I wanted to get a feel for how our ancient peoples responded to the harsh truths of existence alluded to earlier. I have already indicated that to know who you are, you have to have a feel for how you would be if stripped of the modern securities that buffer you from your essential nature. I suggested that our ancient history and mythologies give us some clues. I wanted to see what Irish mythology might say in general about the human condition we have been looking at.

When I explored the pre-Christian history of Ireland from the point of the first human footprint some ten thousand years ago to the gradual arrival of the Celtic language and people around 500 BC, the subsequent arrival of Christianity and the emergence of the monastic movement, I found the same inspirational and uncomplicated truths being revealed in ancient myths, rituals and mystical sites.

Like a dream, they reveal something of the truth of life and what to do about it. Mythology, as we know from Joseph Campbell, addresses the eternal human condition and explores how we respond to the big themes of existence. The psychological and eternal truths that have stimulated our Irish mythologies, Celtic spirituality and our literary heritage can be condensed into seven eternal truths that stand as spiritual standings stones in the background of our lives. Taken together, these truths are an Irish recipe for life and living – a recipe for the enchanted life.

1. Life demands a heroic and defiant response

There is hardly a story, legend or myth that does not have this as a basic narrative and theme. They suggest to us that we have no choice but to live a heroic life. In most ancient stories the core characters face and overcome grave adversities. The constant truth being revealed is that life will demand some-thing heroic, perhaps a grand gesture, sacrifice, adventure, or persistent everyday effort. We see this narrative clearly, for example, in the stories of the early Irish saints. Most of these people chose a life of austerity and adversity in pursuit of a redeemed life.

The inspirational traits in heroic characters are the urge to defy the cruelty and indignity of life and the pursuit of virtue through which one transcends such fate. In these ways ancient stories are about your own life. Characters endure, transcend, survive and fashion some redemption out of what may have appeared hopeless. The characters face the tragic in life and yet rise above it by adding the ingredients of courage and hope. The heroes transcend reality because they, in their suffering, make something noble out of it and endure it with an attitude that forces fate to step down. In Chapter 7 we shall consider how this ancient truth reverberates through your own life.

2. We need enchantment to savour life's blessings

'Enchantment' is a word that appears with great regularity in Irish mythology, folklore and legend. There is hardly a story that does not describe enchantment as a spell or some magical human quality. Enchantment in ancient mythology suggests that one must cast a spell over the desolation of the world to bring it to life. There is not just a magical quality to enchantment; it also has a force and even defiant human quality. People are equal to the ordeals of life not just by effort but by enchantment.

Irish myth and folklore constantly reveal the necessity of enchantment to lift the veil between our fated animal existence and our eternal angelic one. In our modern world of technology, economics and politics the ingredients of the enchanted life are in danger of being lost. We need it to rescue life from depressiveness and desolation. Ancient stories can be read as allegorical tales about you as a reader. They suggest that enchantment must be an essential ingredient in your life. In this way you can hear any ancient mythic story as being a dream about you. In Chapter 8 we shall explore this further and reveal how we transform the banal into the beatific through enchantment.

3. Everything you do in life symbolises something else

There is hardly a myth, legend, ritual or prayer that does not suggest that your actions symbolise something else that transcends them. There is an archetypal and ancient necessity to live a life of symbolic illusion, magic and enchantment to cope with the passion of life and the terror of death. The movement from doing things that are an aid to our physical survival to doing things that are an aid to our sense of esteem, significance and purpose was, as we have seen, a consequence of human awakening. To move from merely surviving to creating an experience that sanctified existence was a huge shift and a quite dramatic evolutionary development. This triggered the development of civilisation where culture and societies exist as evidence of humanity's urge to be more than it is. The urge to a symbolic life is also the source of both love and violence – love being a consequence of inhabiting our vulnerability and violence the consequence of rejecting it.

Ancient myth and legend tell us that we must rise above the unavoidable helplessness of circumstance and live for something beyond this life – even if it is just hope. This is not avoidance or denial but rather defiance and revolt. Transcendence in mythology demands courage. It is the quality of the Celtic warrior – to live and die for something other than one's own self. There is a magnificence to transcendence that is a defiant response to a life that is relentless, literal and at times grim. This is a constant theme in ancient Celtic ritual, spirituality and poetry. You can, like the first monks on Skellig Michael, wrestle heaven from the storms of fate. We shall explore transcendence further in Chapter 9.

4. You live both a literal and a poetic life

Another ever-present theme is that people live in two worlds – the literal and the poetic. You exist in the horizontal physical world of external reality and in the vertical psycho-spiritual world of mythic reality. You have to live a symbolic life because a literal life is too much to bear without meaning and purpose. All of the stories and rituals are about people who move from the horizontal life to a vertical one, from living a literal to a symbolic life. This is the awakening of self-awareness and our connection with the eternal as a response to the transient indifference of life. There is hardly a myth, legend, ritual or prayer that does not offer this message. The thread of the poetic runs through our ancient folklore, is part of our natural psyche and is another motif in our ancient mythology.

In the Táin, one of the oldest sagas in history, when Cú Chulainn goes to fight his foster brother Ferdia to the death, there are long passages of lyrical poems that they recite to each other to give shape and meaning to their encounter. The meaning of nodal moments across the lifespan is elevated and revealed through poetry.

As we have seen in the metaphor of the Celtic Cross, our defiance is our determination to exist within the circle where the literal and poetic realities intersect; where the boundary between the visible everyday life and the invisible one is thin; where the transcendent radiates through the physical world. The ancient Irish believed in the Tuatha Dé Danann and in Na Daoine Sidhe, the enchanted people. These stories remind us that we are influenced by more than present circumstance.

Poetry is the inner ear through which we hear what is not spoken. I shall tease out the manner in which your poetic vision and intuition attends at all of the events of your life in Chapter 10 on poetry.

5. Things are never as they seem

Another ever-present theme in our sagas and legends is simply that *things are never as they seem.* Our mythologies evoke a sense of mystery. They remind us of influences that lie beyond the visible human world, of deities and spirits that influence mortal heroes. Narratives are filled with this mystery and the cause of events is never fully apparent. It tells the reader that this is how life unfolds and that one's imagination must be awake lest one diminish the nature of the world. There is not one story or myth that does not have this as a central theme.

It is reassuring to note that in Irish mythology the kinetic relationship between the real and imagined is a constant. Irish mythology is usually set in both the historical Ireland and the mythic Ireland of the ancestral gods. It implies that imagination, by its radiant light, can transform the earthly things we contemplate. In stories, myths and folklore the suggestion is that with imagination you see through reality, you get a glimpse of something that resides beyond or behind reality. The ancient Irish believed in a parallel reality to physical reality. Celtic ritual and spirituality was inspired through the faculty of imagination, and the way we use imagination is explored in Chapter 11.

6. Your life is not ultimately about you; it is about the life that lives in you

Mythology and ancient rituals point us to the fact that there are forces greater than the self. They seem to say that your life is not just about achieving your personal goals but being of service to the life that is living you. Your life is not about you but about a greater story of which you are a part. This simple message runs through just about all our mythological tales. It is the core narrative of the hero in every book or movie who lives and dies for something beyond the self.

Celtic mythology and spirituality refer constantly to a divine presence that is manifest in the material world, where the spiritual world permeates the mundane; the natural world is a manifestation of immaterial powers or gods. The great heroic stories suggest that if you take yourself out of the centre, if you allow yourself to admit to your vulnerability, you can acknowledge the sacredness of the many things on which you are dependent. In Chapter 12 we will highlight how immanence is very much part of our feeling for life.

7. We are ruled by forces we don't understand

The poet W.H. Auden wrote that we are governed by forces we do not even begin to understand, and this is a truth that is ever constant in life, Irish mythology and Celtic spirituality. An ancient Celt might simply have said that 'we are influenced by the gods who are beyond us.' We are dependent on things beyond our control. Recognising the sacred in nature is a genuflection to this truth.

The Austrian psychologist Otto Rank suggested that psychology or science should not really meddle with this sacred vitality. Science rightly does not attempt to address the order of reality that lies beyond the human mind, the driving force behind all of nature, nor the being of things. The basis for all life is a-rational and is not enclosed by the rational. In the face of the majesty of natural life humanity has created myths and mythologies to give meaning not to external reality but to the inner existential struggles of each person. Each individual person uses the guiding light of their inner mythology to walk this journey. Ancient myths, stories and folktales elevate the nature of life and remind you that your personality is a mythology that casts a spell over the landscape of your life. This lovely thought permeates the pages of the following chapters.

I suggest that these seven eternal truths are an Irish recipe for life and living – a recipe for the enchanted life. Our early Celtic and pre-Celtic religion illuminated the ridge we walk between this world and the otherworld, a ridge walked by Seamus Heaney, who suggested that these are the two orders of reality that poetry seeks to reconcile. Most cultures and world religions create a trail in searching how to relieve this life of suffering and how to touch the garment of the otherworld. In recognising this universal longing and intuition, the next chapters will show how, with one foot planted firmly in the imaginative world, we can live an enchanted life.

Chapter 7

Personal Heroism

Cúchulainn, mortally wounded, received Lugaid's permission to quench his thirst in the nearby lake, promising to return. He then saw near the lake a tall pillar stone, marking the grave of a warrior slain there in some ancient battle. He staggered to the stone and removed his girdle and used its cords to bind himself to the pillar. With his dying breath he gave a great sigh, forming the crack in the stone that may be seen today. From a distance, his enemies were watching him. They retreated when they beheld him standing with the drawn sword in his hand and the rays of the setting sun bright on his panic-striking helmet. So stood Cúchulainn, even in death he was a terror to his enemies and the bulwark of his nation.

Standish O'Grady, *The Triumph and Passing of Cuchulainn*

My six-year-old daughter, Ciara, was tired at the end of her day. After struggling in vain for the fifth time to get the spaghetti to stay on her fork, she let the fork drop on the plate, rested her forehead on the edge of the table and began to sob with a desperate feeling of dejection and defeat. She had run out of the hero-fuel of effort, which for a little child begins to reach 'empty' around six in the evening. She had no more to give and the final failed effort with the spaghetti was the sputtering of her tank running dry. If I, as a parent, began to scold her for crying over something so silly, I would have missed the point of life and would not have seen the effort she needed to keep on trying in a world that does not always co-operate. She did not need scolding. She needed to be rescued from her temporary existential exhaustion, from the demand of being a hero in a little life. She needed to drink from the lake of a pillar stone. She needed to be rescued by another tired hero: her Dad.

Ageless Heroism

When you realise that the story of every movie you watch is a story of someone being heroic, you begin to see that something vital about the human condition is being told over and over again. This doesn't happen only in the movies; every novel or fairy tale is the same. They are all stories of people facing adversity, overcoming obstacles and eventually achieving some success. It is vital to understand why it so important for us to create and hear these stories. We know that we love stories and dramatic movies about heroes, but why is that? What is it in us that requires a lead character to be victorious? It is not enough to say we just like happy endings. Why do we need to keep hearing that courage pays off and that the ending is good?

> Brendan, my son, once announced, when he was very little, that he wanted to watch only movies that have a happy ending! It may seem obvious that a child would want this, but what is less obvious is exactly why this is the case. Why did he need a happy ending in order to feel satisfied by a story or movie? It is because what lurks within a child is the unspoken fear that life may not turn out well and that a bad ending awaits us all. We are therefore reassured by movies and stories that counter this terror (this is why fairy tales end with 'happily ever after'). A tragic ending is too much to bear because it confirms this universal fear. Movies generally must satisfy the human need for a good ending because we know too well our mortal destiny. As we have seen, the literal end that awaits us is death and this dread lurks behind all of our fears. How we deal with this becomes the hidden theme in most enduring stories. It is the stuff of religion and mythology.

The earliest recorded stories, from Cú Chulainn to Beowulf, are stories of heroism. Ancient mythologies and religions all repeat the story of the hero over and over. Mythology, literature and films affect us because we face the challenges of the hero every day. When children report some little event to their parent at the end of their day, it will often be a tale of some small adversity being faced or overcome at school. When you share any bit of news with someone it is almost always related to how someone overcame some obstacle in life. So, while a movie may be about a larger-than-life hero, it is appealing because everyone is facing obstacles everyday – trying to be a hero with a small 'h'.

The world is a stage for heroic drama. The central calling of life, the heroic drive to prove oneself, to make something more of oneself, is the fuel that builds and binds society and civilisation. It is the powerful drive in humanity to be more than we are, to overcome what we are, to live for something more. The heroic effort of people to endure is, of itself, a transcendent response to reality. While the detached, objective observer might conclude that there is no point in trying, the hero defies this conclusion at every turn. Your heroic response is therefore bigger than the reality you have to deal with. This, as we shall continue to see, is redemptive.

Why Do You Do what You Do?

The basic problem of life is how we can achieve a heroic transcendence and purpose. This is presented to us symbolically in all our movies, literature, religion, ancient mythologies, daily news bulletins and so on. However, we tend to deny our need to be heroic because to admit to it would mean we have to acknowledge the truths, outlined earlier, that make a heroic response necessary: that we are not in control, that we are vulnerable and inadequate and that we are forever trying to prove ourselves. However, when we inhabit the truth of what it is to be human, to be inadequate in the face of this majestic life, we realise that we need to be heroic, that our life has to be enchanted and transcendent if we are to do this life justice.

If we can accept that the urge to be someone of significance, to stand out in some way, to feel good about ourselves in a fearful life, are central motivating forces in our life, then the most important question that you can put to yourself is simply this: What do you do to earn your feeling of heroic significance? If you can admit to your urge to be someone of significance or value you can then get a feeling for how you can try to achieve it. If you can appreciate how deep this drive is within you and that its roots are both evolutionary and psychological, you begin to get a sense of how vital it is to you and those around you. You will also appreciate that you can only satisfy this need symbolically – it is not a physical or visible need. If you 'get' this, you will begin to see yourself and those you love in a new light.

We have now arrived at the truth alluded to earlier. To the degree that popular psychology and the self-help movement offer easy relief and simple remedies to the problems of being human, they cheat us of a more satisfying and honest solution.

We repress what we do not like to hear. We feel inadequate precisely because we are human. This means that there simply is no easy solution. Because depression and anxiety are symptoms of what it is to be human and there is no cure for being human, this leaves us with a difficult problem. However, just because there are no easy solutions does not mean that the more difficult solutions are not infinitely more worthwhile, as we shall see.

A Response to Vulnerability, Mortality and our
Ultimate Fear

You will recall that in Chapter 3, which looked at the taboo
against the truth, we identified that the fear of death, and the
other anxieties that are derived from this primal fear, lie at the
core of our psychological predicament, a predicament that
goes back to the dawn of our self-consciousness and awakening
as humans. For that reason, if we examine the universal urge
to heroism in everyday life and life in general, we realise that
its original aim is to counter this dread and fear.

Most human behaviour is motivated by a desire to overcome
our unconscious physical and emotional terror of death by
proving ourselves to be of value and significance, to matter in
some way. According to cultural anthropologist Ernest
Becker, the drive that everyone has to improve, survive and to
thrive – to be heroic – is 'first and foremost a reflex of the
terror of death' and our drive to counter it in some way. This
response to fatalism is magnificently human trait.

From a very young age, children are aware of the problem of
death. They have fears of monsters under the bed that will get
them, bad dreams and nightmares that disturb them, and fears
of abandonment that haunt them for life. All these fears are
symbols of death. No child can name this fear as 'death' but
they will name it indirectly as the dread of bad things happening.
These derivatives of death haunt our fears as adults too.

Given that we exist in a state of vulnerability, inadequacy and
helplessness, we can regard as heroic our refusal to just accept

this passively. In fact, the ultimate heroic act is being able symbolically and literally to face one's own death with courage. Most heroes in movies and literature display exactly this trait – the willingness to risk their own death for some other purpose. It is inspirational because it represents a defeat of our ultimate fear in life. Therefore to face one's own death with courage has been universally admired throughout history. The statue of Cú Chulainn at the General Post Office in Dublin represents exactly this. How to cope with our unavoidable mortality and vulnerability has been, and still is, our central psychological problem and everything else we struggle with is derived from this. And the heroic life is our response and solution.

Ordinary Everyday Heroism

Every person strives to be a big hero in their small life because they feel so small when set against the bigness of life in general. Every child, every person in your family, every patient in hospital is trying to be equal to the threatened anonymity of life and by doing so to be someone of significance. People stand up to life and ensure that they feel good about themselves by standing out in some particular way. The boy strives to be a great footballer; the student, a great surgeon; the employee, an able factory worker. Whatever the small heroics, everyone is trying. Everyone is making an effort – trying to be this small hero in a big life. If you can grasp how essential and vital this calling is in all of us, you will see those you love with new eyes and will understand their symbolic efforts in a new way. Few are content to live a passive life. Every effort we make is our way of strapping ourselves to the standing stones of our own lives and facing what lies ahead with courage.

'I Did It!'

I bet you can identify with what I call the 'I did it!' experience. This is the daily experience you have of accomplishing some very small, if not trivial, goal and the subsequent inner satisfaction and delight you feel having achieved it, whether it is how well you parked the car or making that long-avoided phone call. You experience an inner delight at succeeding at the smallest of things. What this reveals about the heroic effort is wonderful. It shows that life requires an effort that, when it seems to succeed, is its own reward. We are delighted with the smallest of successes and can become demoralised by the littlest of failures. This is because they all represent our ultimate efforts in life. Otherwise they would not matter.

Note the absolute delight in small children who have these 'I did it!' moments. Two-year-olds will screech with joy when they get the block into the right hole, get their shoes off, or successfully close the lid of a jar. Children have an innate satisfaction when they 'do it'. 'I did it, Mammy!', the toddler exclaims delightedly. They are responding to the challenge of life and rehearsing their own quiet heroics. It is inspiring to witness not only the delight in children, but the meaning of similar delight in adults. 'I did it', you mutter happily to yourself when you get all the grocery bags loaded into the car boot. Such disproportionate delight gives the game away about what is really at stake in our ordinary little lives. We play out an epic drama in our apparently unremarkable lives.

This drama can be observed in a nation of people as much as in the individual. For example, the early history of Ireland from the Early Stone Age through the Neolithic, Bronze and Iron Ages is a story of people moving through the country in a heroic drive to discover and expand. The urge and drive in humanity to keep on going, to keep expanding the limits, is truly astonishing and it is the heroic drive of us as a species. Our ancient megalithic monuments, sites, standing stones and stone circles are magnificent reminders of this marvellous, never-ending journey of heroic self-expansion.

Your highest human achievement is to satisfy this urge for some small experience of being relevant and significant – even if it is only doing a job well. We can only achieve this satisfaction symbolically because its literal achievement, immoratality, is beyond us. We do not need to achieve great things, but we do need to feel good about ourselves by way of how we inhabit the little life we have and become heroes with a small 'h'.

The Tear-point of Heroism

You have a highly sensitive intuition for how life demands this heroic and transcendent engagement with the world. When you touch the nerve of human heroism you often reach your tear-point. For example, you will be familiar with the following kind of situation. You are the mother of a six-year-old boy who is at school sports on a sunny June afternoon. You watch your little son running in the Senior Infants race. Running unselfconsciously, he wins the race without even realising that he has actually done so. After the race, he stands alone in the field, somewhat perplexed, and scans around looking for you. And you, a mature 34-year-old woman, in front of the other mothers, cannot stop the tears from rolling down your cheeks. All he has done is win a race, yet your emotions break for reasons you do not even begin to understand.

You are moved when you see your child taking a small step on the long road of life. The tear is evoked when you witness the bravery and hope that makes that step possible. You are touched by his heroism in achieving this very small victory in a life that will pose many greater challenges. You are moved because, however much you want to, you are unable to protect him from the ordeals that await. You know that life will ask something heroic of him.

So you tear up because you recognise that your little boy is rehearsing all those heroic victories and defeats that await him in life and about which he knows nothing. Even if he had come last in the race, you would have felt the same, because life's biggest issues are being played out in this small school race.

So your son runs in a race, your daughter swims for the first time, your father receives an award. These are moments when you see fully what is really there. Your tear-point reveals that you are aware of the ordeal of life and the hope-filled effort it demands. It is your sympathy for the heroic in life – an invisible heroism that is too much to grasp during everyday horizontal life, but on these occasions crashes through you like a wave. This is the wordless ache that lies behind it all.

Feeling Good about Ourselves

The reason we do what we do is to feel good about ourselves. Our need for self-worth, self-value and self-esteem is our primary motivation in life, once our basic needs for food and safety are met: it is this motivation that drives and sustains us. When you think about this it is quite remarkable because it indicates that what is most important to us – to feel that we matter – is something invisible, symbolic and beyond our physical needs. It is achieved through recognition, kindness, or simply being of value in the most ordinary of ways. We achieve some of this by simply working at a job, being appreciated for something, or fulfilling a role. For others it can be achieved through succeeding at a project or achieving a goal; or something as trivial as having a low golf handicap or an immaculate home, or dressing well and looking good. This need will not be denied, even if we content ourselves with trivial accolades. The ways in which people try to feel right and good in themselves are infinite. We take our need for significance for granted and rarely consider why we need it.

There is a direct connection between self-worth and heroism. A great deal of what we do in life is done to counter the anxiety, dread or helplessness that haunts us, and having self-worth helps us achieve this. I am sure that there are times when your own self-worth or self-esteem is low and you fall into the desperate anxiety, dread, stress and even terror that we have been discussing. So our primary motive in life is to feel good in ourselves and we achieve that primarily through the small successes, achievements, commitments and purpose that give us that heroic mission.

Self-esteem and Heroism

Even the small child wants to be heroic – to feel special in some way, to stand out in the world for some unique reason; to feel that they belong and are part of a team or group. Though the reason to feel good may be small (for example being good at handwriting or being picked for a basketball, team), if the child is praised for her efforts, her esteem rises and her sense of standing out is satisfied.

Parents and grandparents know that a child's self-esteem is its most essential and precarious need. When children become teenagers the need is less visible and is gradually concealed, but in the young child it is clearly evident. Because they measure their self-status by simple things, great care must be taken not to hurt, offend or exclude a child. A child bursting into tears over the smallest slight to their vulnerable self-esteem can be a daily occurrence. The astute parent knows how important it is to pour out drinks evenly, share sweets in even numbers, not favour one child over another and soothe the child who is hurt or upset. Teachers, too, see how sensitive most children are to feeling ignored, devalued or forgotten.

While a natural self-value is present just by virtue of being alive, not all self-esteem is a given at birth, like a set of lungs or pair of legs. Children have to go out into the world and learn how to acquire it, earn it and accumulate it. At times this is a huge burden and it creates great distress for growing children. Children therefore need security, safety and love, which help develop their inner esteem and confidence. This is unique in nature. Animals do not have self-esteem problems. Our need for self-worth is our innate need for a symbolic value, to feel that we matter and have a way to be heroic – to stand out or to belong. A way that helps us resist the gravitational pull of our mortality and our feelings of anonymity.

What a difference it would make to all personal and social life if everyone was perfectly secure in their self-esteem and did not need to prove or secure it. The world would be free of conflict, violence, abuse and war. But this is not the case, and symptoms such as depression and anxiety illustrate how precarious our sense of security is; all around us are individuals and nations that feel compelled to prove and justify themselves.

So when your child brings home that painting from school or reports that they did something well, they are revealing their need to feel special in some way, to feel that they can contribute something of value. The child is made visible. It is wonderful to witness this unguarded, innocent wish to be seen as unique and special, to be heroic.

Small Heroics in Adult Life

Our need for self-value, as achieved through heroic effort, continues throughout life. As you read this you still hunger for the simple coins of recognition – a visit from one of your children, perhaps, or a compliment from a friend. As we get older, our desire to feel good about ourselves, and our urge to be heroic in life, become hidden. And when it is ignored or trivialised by others it can be crushing. This triggers the desperate self-rejection and self-defeat experienced by so many of us. In our later years the coins of self-esteem are still being gathered and may be in the currency of the success of our children, the happiness of our partner, the company of friends, financial success, or promotions in work life. Even as we age, we still accumulate things in the currency of self-esteem and significance. Simply being remembered by someone else – a child, friend or partner – enables you to feel good within yourself. Sometimes, you want nothing more.

The main challenge in life, then, is to be aware that what you do is done to earn a feeling of heroism. Everything painful and sobering in what psychology, religion and philosophy have discovered about humanity revolves around the terror of admitting how badly we need this and what people do to generate self-esteem.

A dog, cat or bird does not need to prove anything; they are entirely secure in just being themselves. The human person, however, is tragically designed. As a consequence of our awakening and of our being aware of our vulnerable status in the world, we seek a secure and endless life in an insecure and mortal world. This is the tragedy in life that creates the necessity of the heroic response. By your very nature, you are unsure of yourself, so you keep trying to prove yourself to yourself, others or the world. A tiny robin does not need to do this. Neither does the little dog at your feet.

Because it has had to, society itself has become a system within which, by fulfilling certain roles, people can achieve that need for self-value. By being a butcher, baker, taxi driver, or shop assistant, people can gain a self-status and significance that gives a life-sustaining meaning to their existence. Societies are set up in ways that prove to people the significance of their life. Societies also create meaning and by doing so stand up to life and say, 'We count.' The meanings may be unjustified and dysfunctional, but they show what is at stake for the individual and society. Issues such as unemployment and homelessness are vital not for economic reasons but because they deprive so many people of their need for that unspoken quiet heroic role in society which is so central to human dignity.

Our Symbolic Life

The things we achieve in life, no matter how small, are valuable, not in and of themselves, but because they symbolise our heroic achievement. The truth about the need for heroism is not easy for us to admit because if we do, it reveals two things about us: (1) that we are naturally so insecure that we need to prove ourselves; and (2) that our investment in so many things is less to do with the things themselves and more to do with how they make us feel important or special. We therefore arrive at the quite dramatic discovery that we live a symbolic life. We find our self-esteem in the most ordinary if not trivial activities, from finishing a crossword to getting a text from a friend. That our self-esteem is achieved symbolically and not literally is quite wonderful. It shows that what matters in life is measured in the imagination and not in the literal world. Who you are is not anchored in external visible reality but in your vertical imagination.

This is why we cling desperately to our arguments and points of view and why we rage at those who threaten them: we need them in order to justify ourselves. Why else do people get so upset if you simply disagree with them? Why do we get so distressed over apparently unimportant things, such as our point of view? It is because they symbolise something important to us. They are important because they are a measure of our significance or status in the world. Your point of view is not important as an objective argument, but it is important as a symbol of your attempt at getting a secure hold in a slippery life. When your spouse disagrees with you or rejects your point of view, it can be upsetting because your point is an extension of your self-worth in the world.

It is for this reason too that we react with such intensity over the smallest of things, such as when someone cuts in front of us in traffic. We can rise up in protest over trivial things precisely because we have given them symbolic currency; they are part of how we measure our heroic significance. The more unable we are to feel good about ourselves by natural means, the more likely we are to need others to approve our status by either submission or recognition and the more threatened we feel by minor slights.

The Ultimate Heroic Act

Like all other mythologies, Celtic mythology makes the hero a central figure. The hero who faced death with courage as well as skill and intelligence was deified, eulogised in songs, written about in poems and buried in a sacred place. As in cultures worldwide, the hero was a vital inspiration in the Celtic imagination. Hero stories are not really about the person in the myth, but about evoking in the listener the heroic impulse to be the same. In our ancient history it was people such as Cú Chulainn, Fionn, Oisín, St Brendan and St Colmcille who opened the path for many to follow.

For all these reasons, it is universally recognised, as mentioned at the beginning of this chapter, that the ultimate heroic act is being able to face one's own psychological death with courage. We may all play at it, but the real hero in literature and film is the one who faces their own psychological and literal death fearlessly. You will notice that all of the heroes in movies and literature display exactly this trait – the willingness to give their life for a purpose that is beyond their own physical survival. It is inspirational because the hero has a motive that transcends their fear of death and it is by this motive that they overcome it. Whether they are Braveheart, Harry Potter, Frodo, Cú Chulainn, Christ or Ghandi, if they give their life to something more than themselves, they are heroes. It is in sympathy, then, with the many sacrifices you have to make in life to live for a virtue or value or purpose that is beyond your own self-interest – like being a parent, partner, carer or employee.

Every day in lots of little ways you face death's little derivatives and surrender yourself for something greater. It is a lonely place when this goes unseen, but it is all the more heroic for it. So when you move from a feeling of self-sacrifice to one of service you are elevated. In fact, if you can achieve this, you free yourself of every anxiety and fear that torments you. To face your own metaphorical death with courage is to be able to face the loss of your status, security, attachments, approval or even love in the service of something beyond yourself. Many a lone parent, survivor of abuse or survivor of the recession walks this path, not just with dignity but with something even more amazing – good cheer.

The magnificent trait of the human is heroism – the refusal to accept life on its terms and the determination to be someone of significance in the face of a life that does not grant it. From the small child who stands up and says 'Don't forget about me!', to the elderly woman in the hospice who welcomes her visitors with delight, the magnificent, marvellous and majestic trait in humanity is this transcendent urge, this vertical reappraisal. You are the same – you do not see fit to fold up your tent and give up on life. You endure, you transcend, you survive and you make jewels out of the stones you have been given by life. The heroic response to the inescapable truth of our mortality and helplessness is the redeeming trait of humanity. The primary urge of the human person is to be of some significance, to matter in some way, to count for something, however small it may be. This urge is deeply human and not seen anywhere else in nature.

We can either rest easily and mindfully in our animal nature without ambition, happy to just survive by way of food, shelter and reproduction, or we can strive to give it meaning and promise and to establish a foothold of significance in our ordinary life. Here we see the human need for dignity – the expectation that we afford others a respect beyond their simple animal nature.

Just as nature has defeated death by reproduction, humanity defeats death by way of heroism and imagination. The ordinary hero is every person who rises above their circumstances in life and adds the ingredients of enchantment. The hero transcends reality because they fashion something noble from their suffering and endure it with a cheerfulness that forces fate to step down. The enchanted life does not turn its face away from life's brutalities and tragedy, but it borrows its passion from them. It then looks death in the face and plays its card and, for now, leaves it perplexed. This is the bridge to our next chapter on how we turn terror to enchantment.

Chapter 8

Enchantment

The vision of the artist is akin to the 'enchantment of the heart'.

James Joyce, *Portrait of the Artist as a Young Man*

The Word 'Enchantment'

As part of the journey I took in writing this book, I found myself looking for a word that would capture the essence of our defiant and life-affirming optimism in the face of human suffering and an often unforgiving world. And I found one: enchantment, or *draíocht* in Irish. I use this word not as a lightweight term, but to refer to an unacknowledged mechanism that we use to enhance our lives. I am distinguishing here between a survival mechanism and a life-enhancement mechanism. The former is a physical one that helps us survive. The latter is a psychological one that helps us to enhance life. Enchantment is one vital way we do this.

I see this human enchantment everywhere as I watch how people walk through the forest of their own lives. People enchant their lives with colour, magical thinking and courage. People achieve this in so many unseen and unremarkable but nonetheless magical ways: a family gather around the birthday cake of a five-year-old child; a lone parent decorates her Christmas tree after the children have gone to bed; an elderly man brings flowers to the hospice where his beloved wife sleeps; a small boy punches the air when he scores a goal; a mother tears up when she sees her little girl swim for the first time; a prisoner keeps an old miraculous medal in his pocket; a man psychs himself up before a meeting with his bank manager. There are infinite everyday instances where a person gives a meaning, purpose, virtue and feeling to their solitary life which exist only in their heart and not at all in external reality. But it is all the more real for that. I call this enchantment – the human ability to imagine something life-affirming in their life that is not objectively there. This, as I shall show, is neither illusion nor delusion but the most essential commodity we have – our ability to see beyond what is there and to embellish ordinary reality with colour. This is not at all a flight of fancy but a full, heroic and passionate engagement with life. It is the colour of hope.

What is Enchantment?

By 'enchantment' I mean the way in which people everywhere are able to give their life a magical quality and joy; how they can cast it under the spell of their unique view of life in a way that elevates it above the mundane or meaningless. People do this all the time and it is a quite magnificent and extraordinary thing to witness. Each person's personality casts its own spell.

This is the process of enchantment that gives your life a magic, purpose and promise that are not to be found in the external facts of your life.

> Many of the stories from Irish mythology are also built around magic and are often achingly beautiful. As a result, in Irish stories the energy of reality is allied with the magic and beauty of fantasy or enchantment in ways that evoke a deep familiarity with the plight of the characters. In the dream-like world of mythology, we are enlivened by these fantastical and enchanting heroes and stories. To take them literally is to miss the point. We get the point if we feel their significance at the level of allusion and metaphor. In a dreamlike way the stories tell us that life is maintained and impassioned by enchantment and indeed shattered by the dark spells of others. Most mythological stories have this sub-plot running through them.

Your unique enchantment was not created by reason but by the necessity of imagination. As a small child, you had to create a quietly magical way to take on life. Life gave you no choice. It threw you up on the beach of existence and demanded that you create your own frames of reference quickly. As a child your brain worked by way of images, imagination, desire and instinct and painted the canvas of your life and world. If you observe any little child of three of four you can witness this magnificent process of exploration, creation and enchantment in the blossoming of an entirely unique vision of the world. This is the process of enchantment. Similarly, as an adult, what you see, feel, imagine and experience is entirely unique to you. You are an extraordinary, enchanted and unique person living out the dream of your inner life.

The Inner Movie

Most of us walk about our world living half in reality and half in the passionate enchantments of our own inner lives. Though our inner thoughts and plans are dressed up in adult clothes, we still walk the world with a child-like imagination and charm as we narrate the storyline of our life. While your daily life is measured at the end of the day by all the things you did and achieved, this does not record the inner movie that you have been creating about yourself, the haunting inner dialogues that accompany your daily activities, the reassuring mood music or ever-changing colours of your own day-dreaming, or the heroic purpose that you have given to the moments of your ordinary life. This is your enchanted life.

Your roles, responsibilities and to-do lists reveal absolutely nothing about the inner life-affirming illusions that enchant your life. They in fact serve to conceal your inner feeling for how you are in the world, your inner consciousness of being, your inner loneliness and your delight in the sublime feeling of your solitary life. This is your magnificently enchanted life that has had to be created from the fragments of the world. It is also an illusion in many ways because life gives you no other option. Make up your own story, it says – go on! Do it! And you do. So it is that many people write a magnificent drama around a modest storyline in such a way that their life becomes, yes, magical. Not all the time, mind, but enough to make it shine, if only for a while.

Why we Need Enchantment

We need enchantment because we see the tragic in life. Because life is tragic it requires an elevated and imaginative response. By way of enchantment we can find paths out of the shadow of tragedy, find meaning in the ghettos of life, see beauty in the brokenness and find strength in vulnerability. The very basic religious reflex is itself an enchantment through which we can find redemption and purpose in suffering. We need some form of enchantment to transform suffering. The enchanted and life-affirming illusions you live by are therefore essential to creative interaction with a potentially over-whelming world. The enchanted imagination of the abused child, the imprisoned innocent, or the terminally ill young man are what allows them to find grains of gold in the dust that life has blown their way.

We need a second world that transcends the physical one, a world of humanly created meaning, in which we can live, dramatise and nourish ourselves. As symbolic beings, it is *how* we live an enchanted life that turns our black-and-white world to colour. This is the vertical enchantment of the horizontal world.

If we lived with the full truth of life purely as an animal we would surely die from a failure to thrive, as has been shown to happen to infants who do not know love – who are never held or soothed. To be able to live fully, one needs enchantment and imagination – a secure sense of belonging, a feeling of one's significance, an imagined purpose and place in the universe. If our ability to imagine was surgically removed we would be left stuck to our chairs, wasting away in a narrow and reduced world of catatonic repetition. Nothing would be ascribed any meaning and all that would be important would be literal – our food, our comfort and our repetitious rituals of survival.

If, for example, you are someone who seeks to live and deal with objective reality, you begin to realise that reality in and of itself is a cold, passionless, meaningless thing. If you try to live with cold unadorned reality you will find that things are without value or promise. If you take this to an extreme you would conclude that your life has no purpose, that things in the world are neither beautiful nor ugly. You would regress into animal life and be like the herring gull that flies towards the evening sun and does not ever register its beauty.

Myth and Illusion

The one truth agreed by people like James Hillman, Ernest Becker, Otto Rank, John Gray, Joseph Campbell, Sigmund Freud and so many others is that *we need myths and illusions to live by*. Down the ages, humanity has sought to give a purpose and meaning to human and natural life that is not objectively there. All ancient and modern cultures created their own mythologies about the meaning and purpose of life. This is universal, cross-cultural and ancient. Just as societies and cultures need mythologies and religions, individual people need their personal myths and enchantments.

The universe exists in utter silence. People live and die in billions and planet Earth evolves and changes quietly. Against this background, all meaning is created by humankind. These meanings are not fact or truth, but assumptions about what is of value. We can call these assumptions myths, illusions, or even spells, because their purpose is primarily existential, to help us cope with existence itself, and not to seek some objective truth. Our urge to have a purpose and an experience of being fully alive demands that we create them.

Culture and Myth

Museums around the world are filled with artefacts of the myths of previous generations which we now realise were life-affirming and inspirational illusions. At a social level, these myths or religions ran so deeply into the human psyche that they became the basis of both war and personal salvation. At their best they were the rituals that ancient peoples developed to bring a narrative, a story, a myth to life. They were, at their best, a trance, an enchantment, a good spell, over the life of the individual.

In future millennia society will look back on our culture with the same fascination. Every society and culture creates its own meaning, which in subsequent generations is seen as myth. But these ways of seeing the world were absolutely necessary to create purpose, value and morality out of the ashes and dust of life.

We need a transcendent illusion to embrace the human condition

The need for life-affirming enchantment is inherent in human nature. Its expression and fulfilment is basic to any kind of social life. Only by looking outward and beyond ourselves can we manage to then look inward and embrace our life and death. We are lost when we have no inner balance, no steady centre. To get such centring, we have to look beyond the consolation of things in the world. We do this intuitively and automatically but are unaware of it. We find a heroic purpose, we create a heroic narrative, we elevate ourselves with a light-hearted enchantment and we walk through our day with cheerful courage.

The Implications of Enchantment

Light-heartedness and Playfulness

Adam Zagajewski in his poem 'The Greeks' describes growing up in Russia under the joyless and grim tyranny of Joseph Stalin, noting that the birds and trees were not aware of the harshness of that world and observing that the apple tree on the street where he lived

> ... blithely opened its white blooms
> each April and burst
> into ecstatic laughter.

Enchantment implies this kind of imaginative light-heartedness at the highest level. It fosters a natural child-like impulse towards hope and playfulness while remaining married to a grounded and mature adult imagination. Play, when you think of it, is enchantment in action. If you remember playing as a child, particularly on your own, you will recall the amazing ability you had to create an inner world that delighted you. The same happened when you played with others. You were able to imagine situations or games that allowed you to think, feel, move and exist in a way that had you engaging with life in an enchanted way. We still try to play as adults and when we do we can experience life at its best – be it in sport, a night out with friends, a few pints with a pal, or mischief-making with your beloved.

Light-heartedness and playfulness must not stop in childhood. It still comes to us as adults, but we disguise it to ourselves or else hardly notice it, so automatic has it become. But behind the serious veneer of everyday life everyone wants to play, and still plays with life itself. Everyone knows that this shows the best in us. When we lose the fun and playfulness in life, don't we really lose everything that is vital to cope with existence? Does not the spell of enchantment begin to fade? We know from research with children that if they are deprived of play their development is seriously stunted. Perhaps the same is true of us as adults.

The vertical enchantment is attuned to the music beneath all of life – music that is not sombre or weighty but is at times filled with a lightness of heart, a possibility and a magical sense of how the things we imagine can become true. Then, in innocence and simple beauty, we can sing Francis Ledwidge's lullaby that asks the tired child:

> Shall I take the rainbow out of the sky
> And the moon from the well in the lane
> And break them in pieces to coax your eye
> To slumber a wee while again?

What kind of enchantment can animate your life?

Even as you read this, if you feel you have lost touch with that innocent or playful nature in you, do not despair. Peel back the layers until you find the girl or boy who still skips unseen along the pavements of your life – unrecognised, laden down as you are by obligations. No, your life is enchanted and has an enchantment that may have become dulled, but it is in fact the story that keeps you moving forward. In your private mind, it is still a fairy story in which you want to live happily ever after. Don't let cynicism turn your life into a business plan devoid of anything that makes you sing. Keep the fairy story alive. Begin the next chapter in your life tomorrow with the line: 'And then on this day, something extraordinary happened.' And make it begin.

So when I ask you, 'What kind of enchantment helps you to live?' it is a psychologically genuine question. Freud put the question in terms of illusion. He was spelling out the need for people to have their own life-enhancing myths by which to live. So when I ask you, 'In what way is your life an enchanted one?' it is not at all a fanciful question.

The Myth of Significance

Since the dawn of history, everyone has tried to build another reality that they could live in, dramatise, make sense of and feel nourished by. They began to enchant life, to cast a spell over it that made it liveable. This, I want to emphasise, is not just our universal human quest, but yours too: To cast a spell over your life in ways that animate it, bring it to life and give it a meaning that is not objectively there.

In the great scheme of things, the death of a single ant or leaf in your back garden is without significance. No one mourns or cares. In an objective world, the life of any person is no more important than that of a leaf. And yet humanity drives forward with a shared acceptance that each person has a unique and sacred worth, and this myth has become central to modern life. This is not just an ideal, it is also myth and enchantment. It is a simple example of how we make something out of life that is not there. We create a second reality of human meaning and personal enchantment.

Therefore, in a world of created meaning and value, a world in which you, like everyone else, invest in reality, the life of any of your children means absolutely everything. This is the wonderfully enchanted life of humanity. Through both their imagination and their awareness, every parent on the planet jump-starts reality and imagines their own importance.

The Enchantment of Poetry

Poetry unselfconsciously enchants life and serves to funnel the mysteries of life into the ordinary and everyday. Our vertical intuition and imagination sees so much more in the world than is objectively there. We animate life, give it a persona and bring it into relief, into a third dimension where so much more is revealed. It is not at all fanciful or delusional for Patrick Kavanagh to say that the breeze along the canal was 'Adding a third party to the couple kissing on an old seat' ('Canal Bank Walk').

This same poetic enchantment allowed Ledwidge to imagine, in 'My Mother', how his dear mother was created, suggesting that the moon watched her wanderings with envy and that:

> God made my mother on an April day,
> From sorrow and the mist along the sea.

These simple pastoral sentiments are more than just whimsy; they are the enchantment of a freely expressed gratitude. In his quiet genuflection to the simple things, Ledwidge's enchantment awakens the vertical life concealed in the horizontal life, gives human qualities to nature and expresses a gratitude for

> ... the God Who such a mother gave
> this poor bird-hearted singer of a day.

This is because with the poetic heart, with the soul cracked open, the sympathy between you and others goes deeper than friendship or family, to our shared existence.

The Enchantments of Sport and Music

To find evidence of the power of myth in humanity, just go to a big sporting occasion and watch the spectators. Here is the reality, here are human beings living out of myth. Watch the sporting feats and then look at the crowd cheering. All science, logic, psychology and philosophy are subordinate to this.

It is because of enchantment that sport plays such an important role in our mental health. Sport awakens and serves very basic human needs. Music is similar in that its usefulness is hard to measure, but it has a meaning and place in everyone's life and the way it punctuates significant moments in life is unique. Like sport, it awakens the vertical feeling. Like sport, it reveals the enchanted nature of life itself.

Why do we roar at sporting events, cry when we hear our national anthem, or sing our way to victory (or defeat) at these events? At the level of literal reality, sport, and who wins or loses, is entirely insignificant. At the level of human imagination, illusion and enchantment, however, sport embodies so much. Why else would John Byrne, aged 68, when the local parish won the county hurling final, exclaim with tears of joy streaming down his face, 'It was the greatest day of my life'? He gave reality a meaning and a passion it did not have in and of itself. This is the enchanted and imagined life: Imagining what is real.

The Tear-points of Life

You will have countless examples of events and situations that in the great scheme of life were largely without significance yet moved you to tears or caused you to cheer with rare joy. This occurred not because you deal with objectively measured reality, but because of your sublime ability to give the highest meaning to the lowest of achievements. Your little boy learns to tie his shoelaces, your sister gets engaged, your husband finishes the marathon. You cheer in delight or cry with joy because of the enchantment you have created in your own life. Again, I want you to see how you live a life imagined, a life coloured by you and a life of meaning that you give to the world around you. You! Only you! You make the marvellous out of the mundane! You, with your own passionate and imaginative mind, have made dull reality come to life in the living colour of your heroic vision. Like old Geppetto in *Pinocchio*, you can make a real boy out of a wooden puppet. Wallace Stevens, the American poet, said that we put our trust in illusions – we know they're illusions but believe them willingly. A life based on fictions is possible, he claimed, since we live such a life every day as it is.

We are accustomed to thinking that our lives are rooted in horizontal beliefs and facts about ourselves and the world, but they are not. They stand on the vertical illusions, myths and enchanted narratives we live by. Realising that our lives are animated by enchantment may liberate us from having to deal with reality. Knowing there is nothing of substance in our horizontal life may be a gift, an invitation to the vertical life, to the world that lives beyond us.

Our Religious Disposition

We have an intrinsically religious disposition towards life. The religious reflex does not necessarily require a belief in a particular god. It is the urge to give meaning to something that does not yet have it. Ancient peoples began to engage in all sorts of religious behaviour before they had even contemplated the possibility of the existence of gods. From prehistory the religious response involved such things as art, ritual and symbolic behaviour. It included what might now be dismissively called paganism, superstition or magic, but which was purely religious in origin. There has always been this reflex in humanity to give expression to natural awe, dread, gratitude, humility and the search for consolation. Amazingly, the reflex precedes the thinking. It is how we seek meaning for what feels meaningless. The ancient monuments that lie all around Ireland are dramatic illustrations of this. There is an enormous chasm between what we know and what is, between the known and the unknown, between what we can control and what we cannot. Our attempts to fill this huge gap will always be religious or spiritual in quality. How we fill it is the basis of enchantment.

We tend to believe that we think our way through life. We act as if this huge gap between what we know and the unknown does not exist. We act as though we know what is going on and we like to think that we deal with 'facts'. Yet the enormous chasm remains between what our brain knows and what 'is'. We therefore tend to deny the 'religious' nature of how we fill the gap and instead argue vehemently that our attitudes, beliefs and behaviour are rational. We downplay the free-fall nature of our existence with its helplessness and dependencies. However, the only way we can inhabit the majesty, mystery and evolutionary drive of life with any sense of cheerful optimism is through a form of enchantment. Unbeknownst to yourself, you do this to maximise the experience of being alive and to give your life the significance, promise and purpose it deserves.

As we have seen, we strive to escape the fact that our hopes and aspirations are housed in an animal body that decays and dies. But because we are symbolic people, we are hunters and gatherers of the values and virtues that sustain us – among them hope, courage, love, faith, holiness. We can ascribe an inspirational value to the most ordinary of activities. Because of enchantment, we can experience gratitude for the gift of a day, love others for their efforts to be heroic and find love in the most desolate of places.

So people can tolerate very difficult lives because enchantment brings a heroic purpose and promise, no matter how small. We are able to make something out of life that is not necessarily there. Our life's purpose and meaning are more imagined than real, with each person a modest Don Quixote, living out their own inner drama of importance, love and achievement, imagining their life into reality. However awkward and clumsy the dance, each person is living an enchanted life, finding in themselves the romantic courage, cheerful heroism, light-hearted defiance and radiant sorrow required to draw life out from its seclusion.

The Difference between Illusion, Delusion and Enchantment

While I use the word 'enchantment' in a very deliberate and precise way, as you can see, illusion and enchantment overlap a lot. The word 'illusion' does not include the essential ingredients of enchantment, however – the ability to bring delight, pleasure and a magical quality to the life in which you are embedded; the way it elevates both self and other; and the manner in which it accords with nature. Enchantment facilitates rather than impedes what is natural.

Sigmund Freud suggested that the key question in figuring out how to live is 'What level of illusion do you want to live on?' He was fully aware that in order to survive, people need to have certain illusions about themselves. This is natural and good. If you admit that you need illusion and enchantment to live fully, you are admitting that you are a symbolic and not a literal being. You accept that things in your life are meaningful and important because of the ways in which you give them value. Your ordinary husband can be your knight in shining armour, your child can be an angel to you, the boring parts of your life can have a magical feel. You discover that illusion, imagination and enchantment are passionately human and represent the person who is most fully alive. But, and we must not forget this, we are like this precisely because of our unavoidable mortal helplessness and fate. What is surprising is the denial of our need for enchantment or illusion at all.

I have no doubt that right now, your own life is embellished, animated and magical thanks to the inner enchantment that you cast, like a spell, over your ordinary obligations and responsibilities. However, to admit this would seem to expose the denial we all wish to maintain – the vain denial of our need for illusion, enchantment and, at times, even delusion. There is not a person in the world who does not live by way of deceptions about themselves as people. Half of the people who come into my office for therapy see themselves as better than they really are, as more correct than they really are, as more self-justifying than they have a right to be. The other half feel they are worse than they really are, feel they are to blame when they are not, and are more self-rejecting than they need to be. For good or bad, everyone has illusions about themselves, yet while some have delusions, there are others who find a way to live by way of enchantment, which elevates both the self and the other. These are special people who avoid illusion and delusion and enter enchantment.

To separate the three notions of delusion, illusion and enchantment, I have some working definitions. I consider any form of illusion that is life-rejecting and degrading of others a delusion; an illusion that is life-affirming and in accord with nature is, in my view, enchantment. Enchantment highlights the positive and life-affirming elements of illusion.

Delusion follows what is life-rejecting. For example, all forms of abuse and violence are built on a delusion that evil resides in those who are different from oneself, that one is a victim of life and circumstance, that one is inherently superior to others and that one is entitled to degrade those who do not accept these things. Arrogant people, for example, consider their worldview to be fact so that they feel secure in themselves. Such self-importance requires a certain level of delusion to be maintained. The core delusion at the heart of the abusive and controlling personality is that it rejects human vulnerability and sets itself up as superior and god-like by dispensing fate to others. Delusion fosters arrogance and abuse. Enchantment fosters humility and gratitude.

Delusional people have a problem with existence itself and strive to reject and control it; enchanted people, on the other hand, are at home with existence and strive to accept and embellish it. Both are illusions, but one encourages a person to be more than what he or she is, the other to be less.

Enchantment is the human ability to embellish reality, to lift oneself up, in a manner that has real effects in enhancing dignity, hope and compassion. Enchantment makes you a better person. It goes in a different direction from delusion, while also being a form of illusion. It is actually more grounded in human reality because it rises up from the confrontation of life's harshest truths. For me, it is the quality that defines and redeems us as people. Because of the dominance of a reality-based view of life in our modern technological and scientific world, we need the vital enchantment of the vertical life to counterbalance the literal delusions of the horizontal. This, suggested Seamus Heaney, is the true purpose of poetry.

The illusion that is part of enchantment can be life-affirming or life-denying. Each person lives in their own semi-illusion about what life is all about. They have part-illusions about their own importance, significance, opinions. Hardly a day goes by when you do not meet someone whose view of themselves and their life appears to be off kilter in some way. But when you think of it, everyone has a slightly strange and idiosyncratic take on things – everyone has their illusions about 'reality'.

The provinces of enchantment identified in this book are an evolutionarily based response that enables humanity to move ever so slightly beyond reality, and while they may be illusions, they enchant in a way that supports the effort of life. We cannot live in a literal way because to do so is to reduce the human person to something that he or she is not. We cannot live by bread alone.

The Necessary Illusions of Heroism and Faith

Once it had awoken from the trance of unconsciousness, humanity, driven by existential hunger and need, gradually began to search behind and beyond reality to find the inner forces, entities and eternal constants that transcended it. The wonderful thing is that it found evidence of these not in the world of fact but in such things as virtues, values, hope, spirituality, poetry, music and the gods. And, mostly, in the form of love. Not love as a sentimental feeling but as a heroic surrender of one's own egoism for something or some-one beyond oneself – a giving of oneself in service, gratitude and a faith in something more than biological existence or self-satisfaction. A cynic might say that because you die in the end, it is all a failure anyway, to which I would say that because you die in the end, it is all, in fact, redemptive.

Faith, in this instance, begins to have a meaning. To have faith is to live by an enchanting illusion – faith that things will be okay in the end; that things will work out in your favour; that life is worth the effort; that you are growing and developing as a person. Faith accepts that there is no certainty because the person knows that they can know and control only very little. Both faith and hope are part illusion, but as such, they are also enchanting. Their opposites, cynicism and despair, are also illusions, but because they put the self in discord with nature, they become delusions.

> Celtic spirituality is a spirituality of faith and hope. Many old Celtic prayers and incantations encourage the person to trust in the god(s), to have faith in the generosity of nature. To that end the penitent can repeat the meditative prayer, 'Lord, I surrender myself to you. Take care of everything,' and in doing so, rest so much easier in the world. Prayer is not an act of delusion, as some might argue, nor is it a rational act. It is a cry of imagination and inspired illusion. It arises not in the rational mind, but in the dependent creature, not in the arrogant but in the humble. It is universal, eternal and grounded not in escaping from this world but in being able to inhabit it more fully.

Not only did our ancient Celtic ancestors find their gods in all manner of manifestations, but so too do the child and the poet. They sense that all is alive and pulsates with the divine heartbeat. This is not a deception to avoid reality but a way of seeing that enlivens reality. Our ancient ancestors' belief in the ancient gods and sacred places was a way of imagining the immanent.

A Case for Enchantment

You live a passionate and purposeful life when you discover that the world is a place in need of enchantment. By necessity more than choice, you gradually discover that you must build your world to be a place that can receive and be responsive to your imagination and enchantment. The things that engage you in life are not the objectively perfect partner, home, career or lifestyle but someone or something that can mirror back the enchanted way you see the world. This, as we shall see, is a radical way to look at how you live your life. It is radical because it says that you must not go through life looking for what is objectively perfect. What you must do, by necessity, is to look for people, places and passions that can be a screen that reflects back what shines from within you.

Let me explain. From an early age you cast your own unique spell over all that came towards you in life. You enchanted your world by colouring it from within, using your inner palette. You cast a thin veil over it to give it character. You shone an invisible light over everything – a light that illumin-ated only those things that reflected back the light of your imagination. Those things therefore had a resonance with you. They were the people and places in the world that lit up a little when you shone this faint light, when you cast your innocent spell.

You still engage with the world in the same way. When this happens you feel that you belong. There are places where you feel at home not because they objectively have anything unique but because they can receive you and be a screen through which you can shine a little. It can be a village, a particular landscape, a house, a pub or a place by the sea. A place can enchant you too because you light up for it – it can welcome you and make you feel at home.

Sometimes you meet someone who receives and reflects the very unique light, invisible to most, that emanates from within you. When that happens you feel the better for having met them. Because of this you light up too and, though you never say it, behind your eyes you dance a little.

Enchantment embellishes and enriches objective reality. It brings it to light.

With imagination and enchantment your beloved comes alive; the places that are dear to you light up; the things you choose to do awaken your soul. Like old Geppetto, the wooden puppets in your life become real, all because of the enchantment you cast over them. This is humanity as an aesthetic force – beautifying the world. And it is powerful.

What I want to emphasise most of all is that the perception of beauty, the enchantment of life, the romantic love, the passion of creative or playful activities are not illusions, toxins or contaminations of reality. They are, rather, the ways in which we experience fully what is really there. The world is a cold and lifeless thing until it is perceived and awakened by human imagination and enchantment. When the stars dazzle in the night sky they are made beautiful only by your eye. In the great scheme of things, your partner, children or parents are not objectively beautiful; rather, they are rendered beautiful by you. You do not love anyone based on objective criteria, but on how you enchant them. In so many ways, the recipient of your love contains you. Equally, someone in your life is not objectively bad or hateful; rather, they are so by virtue of what you imagine them to be.

The real illusion is thinking that we must live in objective reality. Ironically, as most people with obsessive-compulsive disorder will testify, objectivity is the ultimate delusion. The more objective, literal and 'real' your life becomes, the more you withdraw into the delusion that this is where you must be. You gradually become detached and dissociated from the world and fall into the depression of the unenchanted life. Depression is what you feel when the world seems no longer to reflect back the enchantments, the spell, the fairy dust of your efforts to illuminate it. And when that happens you begin to stop. Your light grows dim and the gold dust of your enchantment falls at your feet and fades like sparks from a fire.

Romantic Love

Psychoanalyst Stephen Mitchell suggests that love itself is an act of imagination. When you fall in love it is not because the person is objectively the ideal or perfect partner but because they reflect back the light that shines from your enchanted heart. Romantic love is the passion and delight that occurs when both people receive and reflect back the imaginative love of the other. The other person is a place where one's imagination finds purchase.

When relationship begins to go wrong, we conclude that when people 'married' they were under an illusion and that, over the years, reality set in and people see the other as they really are. Let me suggest that this is wrong. Quite the opposite happens. It's not that when people fall in love they are under an illusion and that then reality sets in. Rather, when people fall in love they are living in the full, enchanted, vertical reality. Over time, however, an illusion sets in as people give more and more importance to the horizontal life of security, stability and safety. Gradually people brush away the fairy dust of vertical enchantment and become embedded in the horizontal.

When you fall in love you are actually living an enchanted reality before the illusions of the horizontal life set in. This is why at the point of losing someone we love we suddenly realise what they mean to us. At the point of loss, whether through illness, death or separation, our horizontal illusions are shattered and we remember the enchanted love that we had so easily forgotten and we realise that this was the true reality. Perhaps, if you could reawaken your vertical awareness and your enchanted life, you could see your partner not as they really are in the horizontal world but as you are supposed to see them – as someone you imagined into being and who exists in the vertical. Perhaps, with the eyes of enchantment, he or she may still be your knight in shining armour after all.

When you see what the important things in your life mean, such as your family, you appreciate how your life is enchanted by love and imagination. The same applies to your hopes and dreams. How you imagine these things is what makes your life worth enduring, worth living. You enchant the cold facts of your life with a wonder and meaning that come from within your dramatic inner life.

The Existential Power of Enchantment

The taboo against the truth we spoke of in earlier chapters, which relates to vulnerability and mortality, is really a dread that we might not be able for it. However, the good news is that humanity has always been able for it. The human response has been to move from defeat to heroism, illusion to enchantment, fate to transcendence. The magnificent quality of humankind is its ability to rise to the occasion presented by life and to do so with imagination, courage, transcendence, poetry and enchantment. These qualities are not an avoidance of reality nor a delusion but an evolutionary response that takes humanity to the next level. Humanity developed the ability to imagine that life has a hidden purpose or meaning and to live in accordance with that. This is indeed magical because the enchanting illusions we create defeat mortal predictability and fate. Humanity said to Death, if you give us borrowed time we will celebrate birthdays. If you give us suffering we will learn to sing. If you give us tragedy we will create faith. We will magically bring music, colour and celebration to what had seemed colourless. In this way human illusions are enchantments, human imagination is literally magical and heroism is courageously transcendent. This is not false positivity. It is humanity refusing to be defeated and, at the most basic of levels, elevating itself up the steps of human evolution.

We are in denial of our human ignorance. We indulge our grandiosity and narcissism in a life that demands vulnerability and humility. We have lost our sense of the heroic. This is because we have come to believe that the popular ideologies of economics, politics and science can address the needs of the human heart. Without the rigours of imagination, transcendence, hope and enchantment, however, society turns in on itself looking for a meaning that, in fact, lies beyond in the mysterious, magical and marvellous.

Because coping with life as a self-conscious animal is difficult, we have to break down the enormity of life to a size we can manage. We learn to focus on the little field right in front of us, but when we lift our eyes and start looking around at our human condition we begin to struggle. Many of us spare ourselves this trouble by keeping our minds on those little fragments and we can become preoccupied with trivial things. If we try to take in the full reality of our lives we are at times overwhelmed, so we obsess about these things. There is not a person out there who does not at times feel that they are wasting the privilege of living by spending their time preoccupied with and worrying about things that do not matter. Relationships can, for example, become dumbed down. The romance evoked by the splendour of the great landscape before us is gradually eroded in favour of the walled garden we have secured for ourselves.

But as humans we get caught between both worlds – the horizontal and the vertical. People rush here and there completing small, invisibly heroic tasks because it offers a purpose and significance that the larger reality seems not to promise. If we get lost in that small reality we lose our bearings. We begin to live a horizontal life and break free of the vertical moorings needed to stay at the burning point –

the point where trivial things are symbolic of a vertical life. Equally, if we get overwhelmed by the enormity of life, we break free of the ties that keep us grounded in the real world. We can solve all of this, however, by staying in the real world but enchanting it with heroic purpose, imagination and a vision that makes the small field in which we plant our crops the meadow of the eternal.

Chapter 9

Transcendence

The original meaning of the word 'transcendence' is 'climbing above' or 'going beyond'. The term refers to higher levels of contemplation or virtue that are metaphorically above the world. It can refer to qualities in a person, such as hope, courage or wisdom, that transcend and guide behaviour. It also refers to our ability to elevate ourselves, rise above, go beyond and contemplate our lives as if from above.

There is a transcendent depth to reality that can shine through our everyday life. We discover in places we least expect the heartbeat of life from which we derive our sense of being in the world. There is a part of us that longs for a more intimate appreciation of what you might call the infinite, because we intuit that within the fragments of our experience there is an encompassing transcendent reality that is worth knowing.

Heroic transcendence is the ability of people to transcend the objective conditions of their life by imbuing it with a defiant purpose and a symbolic meaning. In other words, however abject a person's circumstances, they are still able to live for some purpose that enables them to elevate themselves above suffering just enough to help them endure it. Every hospital is filled with the sick and the dying and yet many find a way to be equal to their suffering, to rise above their fate, if not with fortitude then often with a cheerful defiance and inspirational heroism.

Transcendence is a feature of our everyday life. Every day you get up and apply yourself to some goal, purpose or dream that helps keep you going. You take this effort for granted but it is indeed an inspirational transcendence, no matter how modest the hope or dream that keeps you going; it may simply be 'to get to the weekend'.

At the Smallest Level

The impulse to apply a transcendent purpose to living is universal. Inspirational at the smallest of levels, it is common to every adult and child walking our amazing planet. You give an integrity and significance to your everyday life, because you will not take life lying down. You take life on your terms, like the prisoner preparing for his execution who sets his watch to the correct time, cleans his uniform, shares his last meal with his comrades and forgives his executioner. Religious integrity without an identifiable god is truly inspirational. This is a way to transform life, to live for something imagined, to live an enchanted life that does not spare you suffering and tragedy, but gives it a purpose that keeps you going forward.

We do not understand life, why we are here, what our destiny is, or the entire cosmic meaning of our existence. We exist in a physical world where we directly experience only about one per cent of reality. The remaining ninety-nine per cent exists at the electromagnetic, subatomic, neurological, cellular, genetic and physiological levels beyond our senses and awareness. The human brain itself is as much a mystery to neuroscientists as the cosmos is to a child. We are influenced by forces and entities we cannot begin to understand. This leaves us with two choices: to surrender the quest for such understanding and sink back into a passive acceptance; or to engage our imagination and intelligence in striving for a partly imagined purpose, one that enables us to engage with our existence. In choosing the latter, we savour what we have, respond to what happens and walk towards the horizon of hope.

Being a Conduit for the Transcendent

The playwright Tennessee Williams suggested that 'snatching the eternal out of the ever fleeting' is one of the magical achievements of human existence. There is a part of you that can experience and connect with the eternal energies that sustain all of life. This is the transcendent guide you must follow. In the New Testament, the word *kairos* describes a moment when the eternal breaks into and shakes up the ordinary flow of time – when the vertical breaks in on our horizontal life. One might say that the opportunity of life is to be a conduit through which the transcendent shines: every day, in small ways, the things you do are illuminated by something transcendent. The way you greet someone can have a hint of recognition that you are encountering the divine; you do things with the urgency of your mortality and the love of life itself.

The transcendent is everything that is other than what is superficial, observable and temporal. It is how you illuminate external reality but also how divine reality shines through you. When it does you feel like a child dancing happily on a beach, in accord with and aligned with nature. You have an experience of the sacred in the moment, you live for something other than yourself and you have a resonance with the ancestral gods. It is living life with an inner radiance and gratitude.

If you imagine yourself as a gateway through which the transcendent flows, you can live out the myth of the divine reality that is within you. Your life becomes part of a bigger reality than just your private worries and goals. It is an expression, a desire to be a glorification of the beyond. This is a fundamental theme or myth behind the enchanted life. If you see your life as a pathway or portal of the transcendent, your life has a different feel. It is without anger or the need to diminish others.

Parents and lovers frequently have these epiphanies. They realise, for example, that they would reflexively give up their own life for the other. This comes from a deep, or transcendent, realisation that the other and one's self are one and that the division of 'me' and 'you' is not real. When one is in touch with the ground of one's being, separateness fades away. At this level one is living in accord with nature, with one's unconscious, with the reality of one's body, with myth. This is the message of Celtic mythology and spirituality.

Transcendence is about our relationship with both the above and below.

These are lofty-sounding notions, but to work they need to be grounded in your life. And it is for this reason that you need a kite string tied to the wrist of everyday life and to the eternal that flies above – the objects, rituals, disciplines and inspirations that stop us being cut off from transcendent reality.

The 'Above', the 'Beyond' and the 'Beneath'

The formula for a lived life is surely to reach beyond yourself, to live for something beyond what evolution has designed you for, to believe in the enchanted life, a life inspired by something other than what it seems to be.

You have to follow the 'beyond' – the destiny that was the original intention of your life. Your life has to have the shape of your original life-affirming and hopeful myth. You must be in accord with your original character and original enchantment because therein lie the passion and purpose of your life. You must live your life as it was originally imagined. If you do, like any artist, dancer, athlete, or musician, you will be more in accord with your own nature.

To recall what this is like, see if you can remember what your longings were as a young girl or boy of about six or seven years old. See if you can recall the nature of your hopes and dreams when you began to awaken into the world. During those years something essential about your character was finding expression. You may recall what you now consider childish fantasies or hopes, but within them lay the seeds of your own character. So what was it that you longed for back then? What did you want to be? In what activities did you find happiness? See if you can remember because herein you will find what it is that you are supposed to be doing in life. The child in you who lay in bed imagining their life is still there within you, urging you on. But perhaps that child has lost their voice; or perhaps you have shut that child in a darkened room. Think about what you used to love to do when you were about ten years old. Somewhere in that activity your soul was singing. Find something similar to do now.

The deepest eternal truths of life cannot be fully understood because they lie beneath and beyond the level of words. The 'beyond' and the 'beneath' are best captured symbolically in gesture, ritual, poem, prayer or sign. The Celtic religion suggested that the gods resided in the 'otherworld' just beyond our reach precisely because a mastery of our human predicament always lies just out of reach.

Ancient myths emerged from the human imagination in an attempt to express the longing of the helpless human in the face of a magnificent reality. Ancient stories and spirituality were not created by logical thinking but by magical thinking, not by the problem-solving self but by the dreaming self. This is why great myths and religions are as fantastical as they are – they must be. They arose spontaneously, like all great myths, from the imaginative, uncensored and primitive energies of the psyche. The images of myth, such as a cross, a standing stone, a stone circle, a shamrock, a megalithic tomb, are not statements of fact – they are reference points for the transcendent truths alluded to but never quite captured by their symbols. They refer to and evoke the transcendent.

The Ordinary Transcendent

It is worth noting that the transcendent is not remote or distant but something that resides in the ordinary imagination of the innocent mind. When I asked my little daughter what she liked about the hotel we stayed in over the weekend, she said, 'The colour of the carpet made me feel happy and I felt good when I looked at the beautiful stairs.' She did not know why, but she liked to look at them. When you recall things in your childhood, you do not remember grand gestures or events but the small pleasures, reassurances and excitements evoked by places, objects, rooms or smells. You remember the warmth of the living room of your childhood house; the feel of bedclothes at night; the sound of your father's voice; the sensation of sitting on the garden swing; the glow from a fireplace. And all of these things had a radiance that shone through them because of what they revealed and touched in your hungry heart. So the simple colour of a carpet can make a child feel happy because that colour captures all the feelings and emotions that a child's mind cannot ever explain or understand. That carpet captures, in a transcendent way, the happiness of her childhood. As adults we are the same but we notice it less – you like your chair, your mug, your coat and certain sounds. This is the sound of happiness. It is the colour of love.

At school one day, children in my daughter's class were asked what one valuable item they would save from their house if there was a fire. My daughter decided it would be one of two things – a family photograph taken over Christmas, or a soft toy rabbit she has had for years and keeps in her bed. Most children, I understand, selected similarly personal items. She did not choose her iPod, her bits of jewellery, her favourite clothes, her TV or games console, her money bank, or her selection of DVDs. What she chose were little items that connected her with the vertical.

This reminded me of a story told by Austrian-born American child psychologist and writer Bruno Bettelheim, who recalled that during World War II, when an expedition of schoolchildren were escaping from Nazi Germany across the mountains, they were all told to bring one extra item they considered absolutely essential to their survival. When they stopped halfway through their climb, the children were asked to show what they had in their backpacks. To the guides' surprise, they all took out symbolic items like Christmas ornaments, pictures and little prayer beads. These items were considered to be more essential than food, clothing or water. When they were at risk of losing everything, the things the children held on to were symbols of hope and faith that made them feel secure. The magic of life resides in the symbols of a vertical life – in the things that elevate life. The transcendent shines in two directions: from you to life and from life to you.

Divine Reality

The human soul is a mirror of the 'divine'. I use the word 'divine' to highlight the sacredness of life and how, in the same way, ancient peoples found the gods in nature. The rational brain does not know divinity: the soul does. Awakening occurs when we realise that one's self is connected with the ultimate forces of nature. It follows then that if the ultimate forces of nature are godly, then so are you. You and, more important, the person you love, are manifestations of the divine. Whatever you might feel about Christian theology, surely one of its most inspirational meditations is on the fact that each person is an image of the divine. If that was all we took from it, it would be everything – that your cranky partner, your irritating teenager, your idiot boss are all images of the divine. If you can see past people to the essential divinity of their nature, your response to them changes. You just have to get your controlling ego out of the way to let the divine light within you illuminate your day and to allow the radiance of the world to penetrate your heart.

The spiritual perspective is not only timeless, it is universal. Throughout history and across cultures, there are fundamental truths and sacred constants. Early Irish Christianity is an illustration of this. Every god is a metaphor, every way of life a myth, every personality a unique theology, every act symbolic of its purpose. They are all a projection of the ultimate mystery, the transcendent energy source of your life. The constant beat of your own heart, the breath of your own lungs are the rhythm of life and the music to which you create and imagine your own journey and purpose.

Transcendent Heroism

The heroic response of every living person to the ordeal of life is created from the ingredients of imagination, courage and hope. Just as they are portrayed in most myths and legends down the ages, the weapons you take into the battle of everyday life derive not from physical attributes but from virtues drawn from the vertical world. You carry the shield of faith and the sword of courage. A person's poetic, imaginative, hopeful and enchanted responses are not lightweight fantasies but the flesh, bone and sinew of their life. It is not that your hopes, longings and dreams hang like pretty ornaments from the tree of your life. They are, rather, its root and branch.

The human condition is a struggle to make sense of the chaos and cosmic puzzle of life. Placed in this position, each person and society tries to make their life better, improve their lot, endure and keep going with hope and a positive attitude. At the level of our everyday life, that's what we are all trying to do. And we succeed because of the transcendent faculties of ordinary people living ordinary lives. Human transcendence, imaginative living and heroic cheerfulness are not the grandiose acts of national heroes or religious saints. They are the essential and inspired responses of the ordinary, the unremarkable, the poor, the broken and the average Joe.

The thirteen-year-old boy scoring his first goal on his local GAA pitch can feel the passion of a victorious life. So too can the woman who steps back and admires her garden of spring flowers and then retires happily for the evening; the mother visiting her ill child in hospital bringing hope to a hopeless situation; and the retired grandfather delighting in his grand-children. All of them are living quietly heroic and transcendent lives. They do so not because they live in reality, but because they live in the passionate space between reality and imagin-ation (what I call 'imaginality'). By way of transcendence – a virtue that grows from the divine imagination and not from objective reason – enchanted people expand life to be more than it is. This cheerful heroism is humanity at its best. And it is inspirational.

Hope and Courage as Transcendent

Hope is a form of enchantment that allows us to cope with our uncertain future. The hope of the poor, the ill, the oppressed, is not delusion but rather a transcendent virtue that redeems us as a species. To begin to question hope because it is not logical is to completely misunderstand the predicament of the human person. It is to underestimate the need to live in accordance with a transcendent enchantment rather than brute fact. It is a will to endure against odds that would otherwise have us defeated.

Created by hope or faith, this imagined reality is not just a coping mechanism; it is the way we view and engage with life. Hope is a faith in the not-real, the possible. The point I cannot emphasise enough is that we not only need enchantments, we live by them. Before we launch ourselves every morning into the day we have hope that what lies ahead will welcome us.

Human imagination and its life-enhancing enchantments and illusions are created not to help people escape reality but to help them survive and endure it and to rise above all manner of difficult circumstances. The slave who sang while he strained against chains, the men and women who prayed in anguish in the face of genocide, the bereaved who cry out and talk to the departed, the elderly who offer up their suffering to God – all are acts of courage by people fully immersed in the suffering of life. These acts and gestures reveal what we are, but they also make us strive to be more than we are.

Life itself is a struggle between your horizontal focus on reality and your vertical need for transcendence. We hover within the Celtic circle and the standing stones of life, unable to stand as either a wholly horizontal or vertical being. However, the Horizontal Self draws its fuel from the Vertical Self, aligned as it is with both the terror and delight of life.

Heroic Transcendence

The tragic sense of life is this realisation that you are trapped in an ordinary life and a decaying body while also longing to fly, to be an angel. This is the ache of living – wanting to be so much more than you are and knowing that you will always just be yourself! No matter how rich our religion or faith, we are grounded in the earth and soil of physical life. Yet the fire of hope still blazes.

This burning point is the flame, the fire of heroic achievement. Out of this burning comes heroism. It is the point from which we achieve heroic transcendence. This is when our horizontal life has a vertical purpose. Heroic transcendence is being able to give meaning to what is meaningless; give purpose to what is pointless; bring love to what is unlovable; to see life in what seems dead. It is heroic in its refusal to accept defeat and transcendent in its refusal to be imprisoned.

Everyone you see today going about their business is really engaged in their own modest heroism, their own transcendent purpose, their own efforts to elevate themselves out of anonymity, pulling against the chains of fate and circumstance. There are few things in life as inspiring and moving as this noble human heroism. The child dying of cancer dances down the hospital corridor; the grandmother teaches her grandchildren about the flowers in her garden; the man rises early and lays the breakfast table for the children before he heads out to work. Everyone hunting and gathering for the money, food, success and credits that give their life a purpose. Everyone wresting heaven from the world.

Life's passionate tension and suffering is the basis for our moral efforts to do the right thing and to live a life we are worthy of. Being at the centre of the cross, you find motives to live and the incentive to go on.

The Celtic Cross of your Own Life

How you stand within the circle of your own life is unique to you. Most will flee its vulnerability and the courage it demands. Most seek to control the passionate uncertainty, while others will rise in grateful acceptance of this vulnerable life. The motives for what you do and why you do it are ultimately vertical. You are actually always seeking heroic purchase in life because of the inherent helplessness and uncertainty you face.

It is heroic as long as it is characterised by courageous vulnerability and humility. It is cowardly to the degree that it feels victorious in the arrogant degradation of others.

⌇

Evolution represents the efforts of living things to try harder to gain more life, to be fitter, faster, stronger, smarter. We are part of this process. The conflict within us is between our mortal animal nature and our transcendent symbolic efforts to somehow overcome the limits of our condition. If you want to know and understand the human person, this is where you will find the answers. It is the source of all our problems and solutions.

All human activity serves a symbolic purpose. What we do and the way we do it is our unique response to the predicament of life and it means so much more than what it seems at first glance. By necessity, we exist between reality and imagination. And when we are most attuned to life, this is the enchantment of the heart. Every person's singular life is narrow because of literal circumstances, but because of symbolic imagination it is also expansive. You have one simple duty: to be cheerfully heroic in the face of a reality that is relentless, literal and at times grim. This is not denial – it is magnificently transcendent; foolish but at the same time fabulous. You, dear reader, are wonderful because you are able to do this. Right here, right now, as you read these last few sentences, you have the potential to turn your depression, anxiety, stress, or loneliness into something heroic. You can cast a spell over austere circumstances and, like the first monks on Skellig Michael, find the gods in the most desolate of places.

As we shall see in the next chapter, at the edge of the transcendent lingers poetry. Poetry reveals what is hidden in the literal. You and I are more poets than scientists and the very nature of how we live life is essentially symbolic. Our way of living is poetic. We go about our day blessing, redeeming, elevating and seeing into. Just notice your disproportionate delight in the most trivial of things and in doing so you elevate the ordinary. Your poetic intuition is heroic and awakens you through music, sport, ritual, art, *kairos*, frisson and service. And it is to poetry that we now turn.

Chapter 10

Poetic Intuition

Everyone is a visionary, if you scratch him deep enough.
But the Celt is a visionary without scratching.

W.B. Yeats, *Irish Fairy and Folk Tales*

Our Symbolic and Poetic Life

Many books, including this one, are decorated with poetry, perhaps a quote at the beginning of a chapter or a conclusion that returns to poetic language at the end. However, the poetic heart should not be relegated to a clever quote on important occasions, used to create an impression of depth but then laid aside in order to deal with 'reality'. Rather, if we could only see it, the vertical and poetic intuition rises from ground zero of all human endeavours and activities. The poetic intuition reveals the hidden form in the urgencies of life and is the motivation for love and action. It is the guiding hand, the guardian angel of your life.

Every person you meet is living out a poetic life. Each gives a purpose and meaning to their particular life in a way that allows them to walk a few millimetres above the ground. In everyday ways, people are living poets; seeing a relevance to their lives is their response to the anonymity of life. So busy are people acting out their scenes, painting their own canvas and writing their own verse, the real poetry and theatre of life never get seen. But we all live a symbolic life. We give ourselves to tasks that of themselves mean little, but to us can mean everything.

In their invisible and secular way, every person busily going about their day is, like our Celtic ancestors, blessing and redeeming the ordinary through effort. In fact the most poetic of people are ordinary, hard-working folk who enliven the tragedies and joys of living with a wordless blessing. If only we could see it. 'I did it!' you exclaim to yourself when you get to your appointment on time. 'I'm great to get that done,' you say to yourself when you get dinner on the table. These things are made significant by your commitment and effort against the background of a fate and life you do not control.

The Poetry of Life

James Joyce said, in a lecture on the poet James Clarence Mangan, 'Poetry, even when apparently most fantastic, is always a revolt against artifice, a revolt, in a sense, against actuality.' This is a wonderful line because Joyce identifies the heroic defiance at the heart of the poetic life. Humanity did not fabricate enchantment to avoid reality, or develop imagination as an escape. These responses were a revolt that came from deep within nature itself. This deep and passionate urge to respond to life, not to take it lying down, not to be a passive animal, was no clever manipulation or conjuring trick by humanity to deceive itself. This vertical urge was the expression of an organismic desire to revolt against actuality.

If the shoot of an acorn pushing through the dark soil towards the light, the striving of a baby turtle across an endless beach towards the sea, the first push of a baby gannet off the sea cliffs towards flight, or the first gasp of an infant for air could give expression to itself in words, it would come out as poetry or song. If all of nature became conscious of itself and could express its desire and love of life in the face of its terror of extinction, it would not emerge as prose or a scientific paper – it would create religious poetry that was passionate, fearless and tender. The expression of desire, the recognition of its meagre powers in the face of the powers on which it depends, and the terror of its own inevitable extinction and death, would, if expressed in words, be poetry.

The thing is, nature is expressing all of this right now. And it does so through humanity. We are it!

Poetry Itself

Seamus Heaney and the Vertical Life

In his Nobel Laureate acceptance speech Seamus Heaney said that his life's work was devoted to bridging the gap between the visible and invisible realities. Heaney credits poetry for helping the mind to fly and to see the other reality that lies just behind the veil of literal reality. Heaney said that poetry 'can make an order as true to the impact of external reality and as sensitive to the inner laws of [one's] being' as any scientific fact. This is a powerful declaration – that the poetic has as true an impact as the real world. What poetry does, says Heaney, is make possible a fluid and restorative relationship between 'the mind's centre and its circumference'. He credits poetry because of 'its truth to life, in every sense of that phrase'. I ask you to hold these thoughts in mind through this chapter because while the language of the poetic is metaphoric and symbolic, it can be as true as a surgeon's knife in cutting through to the essence of experience. Heaney, in the same speech, said of poetry that it 'touches the base of our sympathetic nature while taking in ... the unsympathetic nature of the world'. Here Heaney describes beautifully what we have been exploring in this book – our sympathetic nature in an unsympathetic world. He captures the essence of the twin realities we contend with: the horizontal and the vertical; the literal and the enchanted. Poetry is an ageless form of Mind-Flight: how one elevates one's self out of the confines of a literal or prosaic existence, to experience hidden truths that lurk beyond.

The value of poetry is its power to persuade you that your vulnerability is closer to the truth than your certainty. It reminds you that as you sail, you lean on the wind of an invisible force that holds you up. Poetic intuition has the power to evoke a sympathy with suffering that joins us with another. It is compassionate.

Thin Places

> Celtic spirituality suggested that in life there are 'thin places' where the membrane between the real world and the poetic world is thin and one can experience the divine by simply being in a place, being in someone's company, or experiencing something. Where this boundary is thin, you are opened to the vertical, the poetic, the divine and to that other order of reality that Heaney identifies.

While people don't read or write much poetry, they do inhabit the poetic world and can experience life through the gateway of what Joyce called the 'enchanted heart'. I am humbled and inspired by the poetic life of someone who lives their life on the threshold between a harsh reality and an enchanted imagination. A poetic place where the victim of family abuse can be sustained by the life she believes is possible for herself; or where the bereaved widower still talks to his long-departed spouse late into the evening. At this threshold people can be with someone who is not there, go to distant places while confined to their hospital bed, travel ahead in time to a place not yet seen and fly to places where they are safe from the sounds of conflict. This is a poetic life.

Poetry both conceals and reveals, but to the degree that it does reveal, it shows the complexity of truth. It is an intellectually and emotionally honest way of accessing the attic of stored yet invisible truths we have gathered throughout life. If I were to ask you if a prayer was accurate, a poem true, or a piece of music logical, you would conclude that I don't 'get it'. We cannot measure these things by the rule of logic or reason.

Poetry, prayer, art and music are just some of the ways we express truths about life that are inexpressible in literal terms.

To the Horizontal Self, poetry makes no sense. Yet to the Vertical Self all things are connected in a deep and integrated way by the poetic imagination. Poetry can say things that are beyond the words of reason or science. For example, in 'The Song of Wandering Aengus', Yeats describes the loneliness and sorrowful imagination of the ageing pilgrim, who has grown weary from wandering the lands of Ireland looking for a woman who eludes him. In the poem he claims that when he finds her he will take her hands and walk among long dappled grass:

And pluck till time and times are done
The silver apples of the moon
The golden apples of the sun.

You live by way of myth and imagination and though the prose of your life changes day by day, the poetry stays the same.

The Heroic Effort as Poetic

We are deeply moved by the nobility of people who, despite the indifference of nature, maintain dignity in dealing with the ordeals of life. To see someone keep their dignity in the face of something that threatens to reduce them to an undignified state is truly inspiring and humbling.

On any given day you can be confronted by indifference and in those moments still stay true to the virtues of integrity and respect. This is quietly heroic. Life and nature can humiliate the person, yet the response of the person to life can be magnificent. For no reason at all, one can bring a dignity to suffering. There is a radiance that shines out from the burning point of your life. As the Persian poet Hafez put it: 'I wish I could show you when you are lonely or in darkness the astonishing light of your own being.'

Your heroic dignity lies in knowing that you are a hunter of values in a world that does not provide them and a gatherer of clues to your whereabouts in a world where you feel lost. The heroic and redemptive in life is persuading your vulnerable self of its significance in spite of the evidence everywhere of insignificance. The search for life's jewels, buried under the rubble of life's stones, is a search that redeems us. Your daily archaeological dig for the fragments of the ancestral gods that prove your sacred and holy life is redemptive. It counters your right to cynicism with a fortitude that defines you and our species at its best. In these ways, every person is a poet and a hero.

Poetry and the poetic reveal the inherent terrors and brutalities of life as much as their consolations. When you are aligned with your Vertical Self you see with a poet's eye and see the narrative of life that explains all and reveals everything. It is not at all the airy-fairy stuff of the naive romantic, the detached artist, or the 'Holy Joe'. This, I cannot emphasise enough, is the scaffolding on which we hang the clothes of our everyday life. Poetry and the poetic reveal the shape of the inherent terrors and brutalities of life as much as their consolations.

The poetic tradition is a hidden virtue in all the great religious and mythologies of the past. Through imagination and a spiritual inclination, you are in touch with the invisible connections that bind all things together. You see how all of life can be revealed in the most ordinary moments. With the poet's eye you see what your own eyes cannot register. You see the eternal masterworks of God in the broken world.

The poetic heart, with one foot in the everyday and one in the eternal, breaks the glass that separates these two realities. The poet in all of us embraces mortality and the terror of death; responds to the human predicament of helplessness; is courageous because it looks for more than what is there; is heroic in that it does not accept life passively; strives for more of a life that is always slipping away; is open to the tragic in life; sees the beauty in transient life; experiences the self as being part of something bigger than it is; sees one's life in the context of history and eternity; looks at those one loves with sympathetic tenderness; and is fearless in accepting the utter vulnerability of life.

Living a life of poetic imagination is ultimately heroic. Seeing life poetically, or 'going vertical', is how the human person responds to and transcends the fate and fatality of life. To do otherwise, to just see and live in reality, is to accept it passively, to shut down the heroic reflex and turn one's face away from one's abject vulnerability. The over-anxious heart moves towards control and certainty and away from uncertainty and the terror of one's own emancipation.

148

The poetic imagination, the refusal to accept reality at face value, the reflex to rise above all manner of circumstances, is not running away from reality but seeing it for what it is and responding to it with poetic transcendence. This is the passionate, full-blooded, heroic elevation of humanity above circumstance. It is knowing your centre while walking the boundary line of your life's circumference. It is not to stand down or to avert your gaze.

> Oh! I have slipped the surly bonds of earth,
> And danced the skies on laughter-silvered wings;
> Sunward I've climbed, and joined the tumbling mirth
> Of sun-split clouds – and done a hundred things
> You have not dreamed of.
>
> *John Gillespie Magee, Jr, 'High Flight'*

The Literal Versus the Poetic Life

The real question, then, is not whether we are supposed to live in reality but in which order of reality are we to make our home? Are we supposed to live in literal objective reality or vertical poetic reality? Poetic reality, impassioned as it is with grounded imagination, is more truly aligned with human nature and the harsh conditions of life. When we examine it honestly, objective horizontal reality is removed from life and is a dumbing down of its inherent terror. It represents a denial of vulnerability, helplessness and the fragility of mortal life and a form of human ambition that is narrow and avoidant.

To inhabit the vulnerability of life takes courage. It is a way of life that has very real consequences. For example, people who are self-righteous, arrogant and controlling retreat from things in life that expose their vulnerability and thus their humanity. Beneath their arrogance, they lock their vulnerability and brokenness in the basement of their life. The righteous often seek to diminish and degrade those who expose this vulnerability. The abusive man will beat his wife for it; the tyrant will annihilate his citizens for it.

The most rational of economists, the most scientific of researchers, the most objective of thinkers can espouse all sorts of beliefs about reality but when you observe how they live their lives you will see how, just as it is for every human being, their actions are determined not by logical thinking but by the pulsating body that perpetuates itself. Just as a seedling pushes through the damp soil and grass towards the sunlight, the human person drives forward. The physical, relentless force of life to keep on living and growing shames the arrogance of the man spouting rhetoric in some pub or classroom about how he motivates himself and how he is his own god.

Many men get trapped in the tunnel of economic success, occupational achievement or domestic control in such a way that it takes over their life. In not having a poetic life, or a Vertical Self that is developed, the only place they feel good about themselves is in their bank account, professional success, at the bottom of a glass, or their domestic control. When this happens their world shrinks as they invest their cosmic status in literal power and control over the people and things around them.

If we are unable to 'go vertical' in a consistent and imaginative way, our horizontal life becomes all the more driven and compulsive. In other words, all our energies are invested in trying to make a success out of our horizontal life because we do not have a vertical life that counterbalances it or puts it into the correct perspective. This is what creates stress in a person's life. More and more of their life energies and self-esteem get invested in making a success of their horizontal goals and ambitions.

> Even the most rational of people live quiet poetic lives. Behind the horizontal scenes of his life, the rational man who is devoted to his religion of reason and progress still finds himself listening to Mozart, walking in the mountains, reading a novel, or tearing up at some old movie. Without admitting it, he sneaks away to the vertical to draw sustenance to keep him going in the horizontal. He dips his feet into the waters of the wild and walks by the sea to remember who he really is.

The problem with a literal approach to life, like science or objectivism, is that it cannot grasp the substance, solidity and reality of the poetic. A literal point of view can deal only with solid objects and observable behaviour but has no language for the intangible forces that shape our existence – our psychological life, motivation, emotions, memories, hopes and the inner light that illuminates our way. The things that influence us on the vertical level are easily dismissed because they are not visible. I have little doubt that if psychological suffering had immediate and obvious visible physical signs, the attitude to mental health would be transformed. If every time we suffered emotional pain we began to bleed, the entire human enterprise would shift dramatically and history would be changed for ever. We need images of invisible realities to name what is unseen. For this reason ancient people had their gods.

A totally literal description of life is, in fact, fanciful and deluded. The literalist who does not want to look up at the skies that shelter him or down at the earth that holds him loses touch with the true reality: our terror-driven desire to master existence and our awe-filled desire to savour it.

The Inner Poetry of Life

You live by the myths of your own unique personality; you engage with the world in symbolic ways; you have very simple rituals that comfort you in the chaos of life; you have an in-character way of doing things that you are loath to change; you sing songs to soothe yourself; you daydream and imagine all sorts of scenarios; and you see the beauty inherent in all sorts of strange and wonderful things. If someone could break into your life and the inner world you inhabit they would not find a checklist of things done or a balance sheet of successes and failures. They would find a swirling tempest of colours, memories, longings, hopes, gods, people and the great forces of a supernova swirling around inside your head like a quantum physics of the imagination or an astronomy of the mind. You are more colourful, rich, deep and flowing than anyone could ever imagine. You are a landscape of ground and colour with fields of light, shadow and possibility. You have an inner culture that is all your own and would be as foreign to others as the natives were to the colonisers.

The incarnation of the existential dilemmas of life are going on all the time. They are revealed in your little daydreams, your minute plans and the worries that haunt your mind all day long. Everything you do is a response to your human condition and the predicament it puts you in. A predicament that is, as we have seen, awesome and anxiety-provoking. The effects of your predicament and how you respond to it cascade down through your life and mind and determine the very nature of your thoughts, feelings, intentions, behaviours and the little things you do.

Grandparents of the Heart

The ancient Irish believed in the Tuatha Dé Danann – the magical tribes who inhabited Ireland before the Celtic peoples arrived. These people were historically beloved though they were likely erased by the invading Celtic culture. The myth states that after their extinction they turned into fairies, spirits and gods that ensured that their influences and their homeland would not be lost to them. The pre-Celtic and Celtic people believed in magic, spells, gods, in the power of the stars, in fairies and the gods of the underworld. It all makes perfect sense as it recognises how a people can be influenced by so much more than the present, than circumstance, than a horizontally objective take on life. This ancient view is devoid of cynicism, fatalism and resignation. It is the symbolic response of people, of imagination, of poetry, captured in this old Irish lullaby sung to a sleepy infant:

> Within our magic halls of brightness
> Trips many a foot of snowy whiteness;
> Stolen maidens, queens of fairy –
> And kings and chiefs ghostly airy.
> Rest thee, babe, for soon thy slumbers
> Shall flee at the fairy music's numbers
> In airy bower I'll watch thy sleeping,
> Where branchy trees to the breeze are sweeping.

It is difficult to describe the poetic intuition because it is like trying to describe a physical sensation in words. Whenever we try to give a horizontal or rational explanation for a vertical longing and intuition we fall short. And despite these difficulties we long for the vertical life to be witnessed and honoured, and Heaney set his work towards achieving exactly this. We need to believe in a vertical life in order to endure this horizontal life and give it meaning.

You might tend to think that what goes on inside a child's head is 'just their imagination', but this fails utterly to see that the child's imagination is their feeling of who they are. If you get in touch with that feeling for who you were as a young child you realise that it was a world of characters, memories, desires and emotions. When you peeked out from your inner world at parents, peers, places and events, you were looking out from an inner animated space, and from moment to moment the reality of your life was as seen from inside this quite magical room.

Your inner poetic world was far more real than the external literal reality. Reality is not 'out there' as units of inanimate furniture but 'in here' as units of living images. Your poetic and imagined life is happening in you all the time. Tommy Tiernan, the Irish comedian, put some of this beautifully when he finished a show with a vignette in which he concluded, 'I'd rather play an imaginary fiddle in the dark than live a life of rationalism.'

We realise that it is at the burning point where the vertical and the horizontal intersect where the toil to the working man becomes a heroic stand. In the currency of domestic squabbles we often struggle with biblical themes. Kavanagh captures this in his arresting poem 'Epic', about a row between neighbours, which tells of how he was losing faith in humanity until Homer's ghost came whispering and said:

> I made the Iliad from such
> A local row. Gods make their own importance.

And when we are awakened to the vertical dimension in all of life, the sorrow of the soul and the joy of the heart, we see all things with such radiant sorrow that it quickens every encounter and every horizontal problem. The poet in you senses and knows this. Your poetic ear quickens your joy but always with the ache of vulnerability. So we must, as Ledwidge wrote in his poem 'June':

> Joy in it and dance and sing
> And from her bounty draw her rosy worth.

Because, again, we are attuned to the vertical grief of life that attends all things, we must rise above life a little so that we can see down the road on which we all travel, because otherwise we take it all for granted. We must grasp the moment because when we can lift our head we see, like Ledwidge, that:

> Even the roses split on youth's red mouth
> Will soon blow down the road all roses go.

Chapter 11

Imagination

In imagination only we find a Human Faculty that
touches nature at one side and spirit on the other.
W.B. Yeats, *William Blake*

Imagination as a Unifying Concept

All roads lead us to the central unifying force that is the human imagination. Psychology, philosophy, theology, poetry, neuroscience, history and the human story all intersect around this human faculty. The basic unit of the mind, of our thinking, is not a thought but an image. And human imagination is the multidisciplinary centre point that brings everything together. Of all our faculties, it is the jewel in the crown. While all the disciplines and arts offer different perspectives on human life, they all agree on the central place of imagination.

Imagination is the faculty of forming images of what is not actually present to the senses. By definition, this refers to almost all of our psychological life. Most of what goes on in our heads is a form of imagining and represents about ninety-eight per cent of our mental life. What most people consider to be thinking is really imagining. It enables us to imagine what does not yet exist and then to move forward into the future. Our ability to imagine is the oxygen of our mental life. Imagination is the electrical current of mental activity; it is the battery charge of your mental life. 'Imagination is more important than knowledge,' said Einstein, 'For knowledge is limited to all we now know and understand, while imagination embraces the entire world and all there ever will be to know and understand.'

Imagination as Advanced Cognition

The human imagination is one of the most advanced and sophisticated cognitive instruments. It is the most powerful and incisive problem-solving tool at our disposal. Far from being something lightweight or trivial, it is central to how we represent and manipulate the world and how we plan the future. We use our imagination to solve every kind of problem. How am I going to get those things done in the time I have? How much money will I need over the weekend? What will I say to my mother when I ring her later? How do I unravel this knot? Every single problem is solved through imagination because to solve a problem you have to be able to conceive of something that has not yet happened.

The ability to imagine something is the basis of all thinking and problem solving. Ninety-eight per cent of our daily thoughts are examples of active imagination, from foresight

('I'll go to the shop later to get food') to the sorrow we feel at the thought of losing someone we love.

Imagination is critical to child development. This can be seen in children's love of novelty; their use of fantasy; the way they engage in pretend play and their ready ability to personify inanimate objects. Children, before they have learned to speak or do anything, are already beginning to imagine their world through their body. By being able to physically influence things, they anticipate how they might influence the world. This anticipation requires imagination.

Imagination is also essential to a child's sense of the constancy of things they cannot see. For example, a child has an inner image of 'Mom' or 'Dad' that they carry around with them and that makes them feel secure, particularly when Mom and Dad are not present. The discovery of person constancy, that people continue to exist in imagination when not seen, is a significant cognitive step in child development. The one-year-old child does not need to see Mom to know that she is in the next room. The baby can call up the image and feel safe.

To be without imagination in adult life would be to be severely autistic, to the point of being unable to connect with the world. Michelangelo said that perception is secondary to imagination, while Einstein claimed that imagination is more powerful than intelligence. In saying these things, these great thinkers were not being romantic but acknowledging imagination as the tool that enables us to progress into the future. Your imaginative intelligence is what ultimately choreographs and shapes your life. Human imagination is the assertive, problem-solving, solution-creating, evolution-based ability of humanity to make so much more out of reality than is already there.

While the information we rely on in the modern world comes from science, economics, politics and law, most of the activity inside the heads of people going about their day-to-day life is grounded in imagination. If we could get a glimpse of your inner world we would not find a library of facts but billions of neurological worker ants creating reality in a kaleidoscope of colour and activity.

The development of *foresight* in the human being changed everything in human evolution. It meant that the moments, days, months and seasons that lay ahead could be considered and created in people's imagination. In reality, nothing ahead of us yet exists. It has all to be imagined. The human animal has evolved into a being that, unlike all other animal life, survives and thrives exactly because of this exceptional cognitive imagination. Over time, the imagination has become to the human being what a keen sense of smell is to the hound, what speed it to the cheetah, what height is to the giraffe, what stealth is to the big cat. That's what we do – and it both enlivens life and makes us equal to it. This imaginative foresight is what makes you different from the cow in the field that is contentedly just living for the present.

At some point during the latter stages of human evolution, nature selected those lineages with a predisposition to be able to imagine alternative realities. To survive and to overcome the limitations of the finite physical reality and the pain, suffering and death it caused, the earliest humans had to imagine a different reality. This is how tools were invented. Through imagination new realities were born that enabled humans to transcend, to imagine that they could be different from what they were. Humans had to imagine bridges, wheels, tools, clothes and other objects before they could create them. But imagination applies to higher virtues, too, like fortitude and hope.

Imagination and Life

We live our life primarily in our heads. That is where everything of importance dwells. It is as simple as that. The physical world itself exists as pure being – without motive or reason. Before we arrived on the planet, nothing required meaning, value or purpose. However, humanity as a species created meaning and the savouring of experience. Each person expresses this through the rituals, myths and illusions of everyday life. Our ability to savour life itself develops in the greenhouse of human imagination. We do it through a sense of narrative and gratitude. We savour and give meaning to life through literature, poetry, movies, culture, sport and all sorts of social rituals such as birthdays, weddings, wakes or graduations; and through little genuflections to everyday life – greetings, goodbyes, affirmations and the barely noticed encouragements we offer to one another.

Imagination enables us to live a richly symbolic life. In fact language itself is a system of symbols.

Reason and imagination do depend on one another, however. Our imagination must stand at the burning point between the horizontal and the vertical, between concrete fact and human imagination. Imagination is the connection between the visible and the invisible – it is the river that flows beneath them.

It is reassuring to note that in ancient Irish mythology the relationship between the real and imagined is constant. This mythology is set in both the historical Ireland and the mythic Ireland of the ancestral gods. Many of the characters are godly mortals, so it is not easy to tell divine from human. This is in fact an entirely appropriate representation of the nature of life. Past and present, myth and reality, are always mixed in Irish mythology, folklore and ritual. And this is how it should be in any poetic text that seeks to reveal the invisible enchanted truths I am writing about. I am trying to express in a literal way what these ancient stories revealed to their listeners in a symbolic way. A child who hears a myth hears the simple story that there is more going on in life than is apparent to the naked eye. In itself, this is a wonderful endorsement of a child's inner life.

Your imagination, by its radiant light, enchants and enlightens all the earthly things you contemplate. Through imagination you get a glimpse of something hidden behind reality. It is entirely reasonable to say that the imagination opens the processes of enchantment like a window to the divine.

The ancient Irish believed in a parallel reality that existed alongside physical reality, a world the hero might enter to gain wisdom, or from where an ancestral god might visit an ordinary person in distress. In poetic ways, ancient myths spoke about these kinds of eternal truth. Truths that were revealed in dramatic heroic tales that helped the suffering person alter their own view of their life. This was acknowledged in small but significant enough ways to help them endure the hardship of life. And when the imagination of the heart is opened you find God in the ordinary and, to quote Heaney's encouragement, when you listen intently to something as simple as the sound of water, 'You are like a rich man entering heaven' ('The Rain Stick').

A Symbolic and Imaginative Life

President Michael D. Higgins laid a wreath at the Grave of the Unknown Soldier in England. Queen Elizabeth laid a wreath at the Garden of Remembrance in Ireland. We tend to think of these as just grand symbolic gestures, but your entire life is, in fact, like a series of small symbolic gestures, rituals and declarations that, like the President's gesture, hint at the unspoken reality of your life. Even a greeting or a goodbye is laden with meanings you dare not speak. A conversation with one of your children, a phone call to a friend, an effort to do something well are significant because behind them lies a world of meaning that the gestures themselves both conceal and partly reveal. In every day of your life your actions and deeds are symbolic of something that lies just beyond your awareness and understanding.

However, when you get anchored in an imaginative appreciation, you are not only aware of it, you see it with such brilliant clarity that it can be awesome – as if the curtains have parted and you see the drama and pathos of each person's individual life. It is an awareness that allows an imaginative appreciation of the toil of a lone parent carrying home the shopping, the dignity of the postman on his round, the glee of the child playing football on the green, the contentment of the grandmother pruning her rose bushes, the grief of the couple in the maternity unit, the terror of the young woman going for her first job interview, the determination of the thief breaking a window into a flat. Everyone is seeking a feeling of significance and control in a life that guarantees neither.

Your experience of life and your everyday struggles and problems are never literal and always symbolic of a heroic effort. Your personal life is a unique way in which one human acts out and reveals, in physical form, their solution to the impossible equation posed by life itself. The objective realities of your life are the ways you choose to walk into the storms of life and across the wondrous landscape laid out before you. Life is not just *like* a dream or a heroic drama; it *is* these things. The imaginative approach to life is not just a fancy way to talk about life but is, in fact, the most physical and basic way.

The imagined life we live behind the curtains of our everyday activity must be appreciated. Imagination is the way in which our vertical life finds expression. The vertical mist of the soul condenses on the walls of our inner life as the water of imagination. Our imagination is the medium through which our silent and wordless life finds expression.

All Human Activity Serves a Symbolic Purpose

Scientists, neurologists and evolutionists do not seem able to grasp the existential emergency that shapes people's attitude and relationship to the world. This 'emergency' is psychological more than biological and affects human life in ways that the physical sciences cannot fathom.

The profound conclusion is that all human activity serves a symbolic purpose. By necessity, we exist between reality and imagination, in the realm of what I call 'imaginality'. Every person's singular life is narrow because of literal circumstances, but because of symbolic imagination it is also expansive. The symbolic purpose of human life is rarely seen by the archaeologist or neuroscientist – they examine a necessary but different order of truth. (I was recently taken aback when I read a history of the archaeological finds of pre-Christian Ireland that had not one reference to the likely psychological, existential or spiritual imperatives that made the creation of the archaeological items by Neolithic people necessary and meaningful.)

The Little Things

Symbolic Imagination Enchants the Real World

Because of symbolic imagination, the young woman working at minimum wage to care for her two little children lives a heroic and transcendent life unknown to the wealthy heiress dining on her yacht in Monte Carlo. The boy scoring his first goal on his local soccer pitch can feel the passion of a victorious life just as intensely as Lionel Messi scoring for Barcelona in a big league game. The mother visiting her ill child in hospital every day, the son visiting his father in the cancer unit every morning, the retired grandfather babysitting his grandchildren three nights a week – they are all living heroic and transcendent lives not because they live in objective reality, but because they live slightly beyond it, in the passionate world of 'imaginality', where people imagine their lives with gratitude and compassion. Imagination is essential to thrive and be content.

Our Disproportionate Delight with Trivial Things

As human beings we often feel good about ourselves for the smallest and most insignificant of events or successes. People can be thrilled beyond measure by achieving something like getting a wardrobe to fit neatly into a corner or painting a skirting board without getting paint on the wall. Our self-esteem and moment-to-moment positivity can be affected by the smallest thing. And equally, the tiniest personal failure or defeat can trigger a disproportionate negative reaction. Your mood can plummet because of someone's tone of voice or because you spot your spouse eating with their mouth open. For the most trivial reason, we can find ourselves feeling disproportionately irritated, defeated or depressed. To find that we are symbolic people who have symbolic meanings for everything we experience in the outer world is a dramatic revelation. To decode what these little events represent for us can be astonishing.

Because we do it all the time, it is worth thinking about the symbolic value we place on ordinary achievements. It conceals a quite profound truth about how we elevate the ordinary. That all our little achievements affect us so much is because we are symbolic people, and everything we experience in the outer world has an inner symbolic meaning and value. Our days are filled with constant fluctuations in our mood, self-esteem and confidence as we fail and succeed at the tasks we set ourselves. We grossly underestimate the power of the smallest achievement to counter the subconscious feeling of impotence and inadequacy that haunt our species. This inadequacy stems from our unavoidable existential helplessness. Yet because of it we can have the wonderful little experiences of success that seem to say 'I do matter'. It is magical, really. Unless we felt unimportant we would not know the delight of success. Unless we felt hopeless we would not know the inspiration of hope.

Everything you feel and think is not real in any physical sense: if we cut open your brain we find no evidence of anyone in there – all we find are blood, flesh, cells, nerves and globs of neurons. There would not be one tiny shred of evidence in your brain that would distinguish yours from anyone else's. No photographs no memories, no sounds, no experiences and no stories. Nothing. Only the silent flesh of the brain. It's a rather obvious illustration but one that shows that the reality in which you live is all imagined. An encoded symbolic inner mysterious world.

Ue Need Sacred Objects to Symbolise the Eternal

Celtic people, indigenous forms of spirituality and many forms of traditional religion have physical objects that symbolised and received the deities. They were the dwelling places of the gods. For Celtic people it could be a standing stone, a sacred well, a woodland or a piece of jewellery. Irish legend is filled with references to objects or places that served as the conduit through which the magical or eternal was revealed. According to legend, the Celts had the 'four hallows' which belonged to the gods and were thought to bring well-being to Celtic lands – the Sword of Nuada, the Spear of Lugh, the Cauldron of the Dagda and the Stone of Destiny. Most ancient cultures had similar talismans.

If you think believing in a holy medal or sacred place is just superstitious you fail to see the many things in your life that have assumed a similar talismanic effect and disproportionate influence on your well-being – perhaps a photograph, an old letter, a card from someone special or a family heirloom. You explain it away as simple sentiment, but if you were to lose the 'sentimental' object you would be quite upset. You probably have some items like this with you right now that you pay little heed to but that nonetheless make you feel safe – something like, perhaps, a wedding ring. Your home is probably decorated with symbolically meaningful objects that genuinely give you a feeling of connection with someone or something that is departed. As a human being, you actually need personal objects that serve a symbolic purpose for you. They give added meaning to your life. These items keep the sacred alive in a real way. They help you to stay in touch with the essentials of your poetic life while you go about the business of your literal one. A prayer on your dashboard, a holiday snap on the window sill over the kitchen sink, a child's photograph hidden in your purse – all these things are more than sentiment. They make you feel worthy because without them you might doubt that worth. They keep your imagination alive.

Childhood Imagination

Children assign human attributes to inanimate objects in a very natural way; this is called anthropomorphism. Watching children engage in pretend-play reveals how the human mind naturally imbues things with human qualities. Children believe readily that teddy bears are real, that ghosts and spirits exist, that guardian angels watch over them and that animals are like humans. This imaginative engagement with life is not idle or insignificant – in fact it is filled with a magical meaning that stays with a person all their adult life. It remains with you precisely because it connects with a longing that is so deep in your nature that you never forget the magical experiences of childhood, while you will hardly remember the literal. You remember Christmas Eve with such fondness because it got closer to the heart of life than anything else. It may seem silly in retrospect, but it is not. It cuts to the deepest part of the human person. For this reason adults all over the world want to recreate those magical experiences for their own children not because it was a trick played on them but because it awakened in them a way of being in the world that was, and still is, enchanting in every courageous meaning of that word.

This connection with the magical and divine gets repressed, cut away or hidden as people get older. It gets channelled into more acceptable forms of adult animation, such as sport, watching TV and other forms of adult play that masquerade as something sensible. We follow a flag, team or celebrity with the same kind of 'imaginality' as a child. The problem is that we do not realise it and we pretend that we are now driven by reason rather than soul.

Hope is a real example of a belief in more than reality and how we can move beyond it. If you argue that we must accept reality just as it is, you argue that there is no need for hope. Hope is entirely an imaginative virtue. And we need such life-enhancing illusions and virtues to propel us forward.

Your imagination is what makes love possible. In this way your hard-working, loyal, slightly overweight husband can be your knight in shining armour; your daughter can be your uncrowned princess. The ordinary lives of those you love can be appreciated as being wonderfully heroic.

Imaginality: Reality Plus Imagination

> Two men looked out through prison bars;
> The one saw mud, the other stars.
>
> Anon.

I can say with some confidence that you are not supposed to live in reality. In fact reality, as a concept, is over-rated. Most of us are brought up thinking that if we are to get on in life we must live in the real world, yet without fleshing out what the 'real world' is. We believe we should be 'real'-istic. Now of course this is essential, but only on the matter-of-fact and 'horizontal' level. We have to exist in that world of reality but, as you have gathered, that is only one dimension. One of the essential points of this book is that for scientific, biological, evolutionary and psychological reasons we are not supposed to passively accept the hard facts of external reality. For evolutionary reasons alone, the force of nature that drives us on, making efforts every day to be better, actually requires a refusal to accept reality. The imagination is, as Joyce suggested, a revolt against actuality. Just as an acorn buried deep within the earth fights through mud and the weight of soil to break the surface to seek out light, with imagination we try to push the weight of reality aside to break through to the light of passion and purpose. Your life is a heroic refusal to accept reality. It is a determination to transcend it and, in doing so, to give a glorious meaning to your everyday existence.

We exist in imagined realities, such as love, self-esteem, confidence, hope, goals, meaning, purpose or status. Imagination-based thinking is how the mind functions. Animals exist much more in physical reality. The further down the evolutionary scale you go, the more animals are guided by stimulus–response reflexes and pure instinct. A cow in a field never thinks, 'I wish I were a horse.' Her physical existence and 'cow-ness' is all there is. There is no imagined life. It is the same with every other animal – except the human.

Imagination is what allows us to engage with, and be embedded in, physical reality in an active and involved way.

Your active life is therefore not in the physical world but in the imagined and enchanted world. Everyone is watching a different internal movie, recollecting different things and experiencing a reality that is enchanted, magical and imaginative. It's all *in there* and it is all *imagined reality*. All of our emotional problems exist only in the form of human imagination – in the symbolic images, myths and beliefs that reside between our ears in the form of electrical impulses and neurological activity. And while the outer objective world stimulates this inner symbolic world into life, it is the latter world that takes primacy.

Imagination and Problem-solving

We inhabit a world of imagination and reality. What we consider to be reality is what is physically present, here and now, like a rock-hard fact, a verifiable truth, an observable entity or phenomenon. We therefore think that anything else is some form of illusion. However, we do not inhabit the world of rocks and objects – we inhabit the vivid, vital world of the mind and imagination. Rock-hard reality is passionless and cold. Animated reality is imagined and passionate. We only have 'imaginality' – reality plus imagination. Objective reality represents only a tiny portion of human reality. The physical reality 'out there' is just the hook on which we hang the coats of our inner lives, the canvas on which we paint our story. When you think or imagine things, nothing happens in physical reality – there is no record anywhere of it – but in your imagined reality, a lot has happened.

Imagination has ensured that as a species we have survived a wide variety of physical circumstances, from the frozen wilderness of the Arctic to the baking heat of the Sahara, simply because it has allowed us to conceive of a different reality in which existence in such harsh environments could be achieved. We do not live in the Here and Now, we live in the magical space between the Here and the There, between the Now and the Then. We can *imagine things that do not exist* and we can transform those dreams into reality.

It's important not to romanticise the imagination because the same imagination creates fears, phobias, anxiety, depression and stress. So I have no illusions that the cause of problems is often an overactive imagination. However, the antidote to negative imagination is not rationalism – it is positive imagination.

Positive Imagination

When a child is asked to spell a word like 'believe' they need to be able to draw up an image of the word to visualise it and then spell it out. This is an act of imagination. When they are taught about the planets and solar system, without ever having seen them, they have to imagine these things in their heads before understanding them. When they have to figure out a physical problem, such as the old brainteaser of how the farmer gets the fox, chicken and grain across the river, they solve it in their imagination.

In fact, if you think of any human problem solved by thinking, you realise that imagination, the ability to imagine things that do not exist, is the engine of all problem-solving. Every day, our extraordinary brains imagine all sorts of scenarios in order to figure out what to do with the myriad problems we face. In fact most of our life is spent in the imaginary world of our mental life as we recall, plan, analyse, consider and so on.

All thinking is therefore imaginary. All great discoveries and inventions have been achieved by the hunger of human beings to imagine new possibilities. Inventing anything, from a paper clip to a computer, is only possible by way of imagination.

At another level, the whole drive of evolution, which allows species to advance their own development, requires a vague sense of something more, something else. In studying the Irish people from when the first Stone Age person set foot on Ireland about 8000 BC through to this day, you get a dramatic sense of the movement of people over millennia across Europe to the outer reaches of the west of Ireland. Why? This movement, growth and development was driven by their imagination – the desire to be somewhere better than where they were.

In our personal life, positive imagination facilitates courage, happiness, goal setting and progress. It is also integral to human emotions like recollection, grief, hope and dream-making. It is not an embellishment at the edge of the real world. It is, rather, the currency through which we engage with the world and do something about it. Without imagination we become 'autistic' or disengaged, stuck in a literal, prosaic world of stimulus and response, repetition and inertia. Even getting out of one's chair to make a cup of coffee and a sandwich is made possible by how your brain imagines it in the first place. If you are stuck in the moment and can process only the data that comes to you from reality, you hardly move. You are like a computer, subject to how you are programmed. As human beings, however, we are forever trying to step outside our current programming, pushing forward, exploring and rising above.

The Distrust of Imagination

There has always been a distrust of imagination because of the tendency to align it alongside delusion and fantasy.

Imagination has always been downgraded as the poor relation of intelligence and often classified as something that avoids reality. People refer to imagination as a lesser cognitive function: 'You're just imagining things,' 'That's all in your imagination,' 'Deal with reality.' We tend to associate a rich imagination with under-achievers like day-dreamers, fantasists, artists and the like.

However, imagination is the unifying faculty of mental life. The imagination draws disparate data into a coherent whole and gives meaning and sense to disconnected facts; it is the means by which we engage with reality and do something with it. Relentlessly active and seemingly limitless in its capacity, imagination is the creative engine of the mind.

Your own inner life is a fluid dream-like river of images, thoughts, memories and information – a flow of consciousness that tumbles and leaps forward in a colourful explosion of insights, ideas and imaginings. Your inner life is a symbolic, poetic, artistic, sensory, idealistic, erotic and passionate one that churns up from your unconscious like a bubbling cauldron of moment-to-moment consciousness. At any given moment in your life, the flowering of sensuous imagination and emotional ideas is quite magnificent.

Chapter 12

Immanence

Bidden or unbidden, God is present

Carl Jung

I mmanence refers to a divine presence manifest in the material world; it is where the spiritual world permeates the physical. It refers to how the natural world and creatures are a manifestation of an entity, god or force whose original nature is non-material. It complements the idea of transcendence, in which the divine is seen to radiate through the material world.

If you allow yourself to admit to your littleness, you know you are just like a leaf from the tree of a great forest, dependent on many things greater than you that sustain your life – water, energy from the sun and oxygen from the air. These would be your gods. In life we are no different.

The Metaphor of the Celtic Gods

The senses and imagination precede thought. Hence the saying, 'It has to be seen to be believed.' Eating a chilli pepper reveals more truth than trying to describe one. The gods in Celtic and ancient traditions were sensed before they were thought of. They did not exist because they were thought up to explain something – they existed because the mysterious forces, entities and powers of life and nature were *sensed* by people. Though the gods do not exist in a scientific sense they are eternally true in a poetic and mythic sense.

As I have argued, poetic vision is necessary and essential to a fearless and honest life that accepts the necessity of heroic imagination. A literal life is not worth living because it turns its face away from what it cannot understand. What does it matter if you call them gods, nature, cosmic order, or the miraculous force of evolution? The metaphors are secondary to the reality – a reality that is revealed as much by science as by mysticism. A flick through *Scientific American* or *National Geographic* offers as many glimpses of the wonder of life as the Old Testament or the Upanishads, the sacred Hindu texts. Whatever door you enter, you experience the miracle and majesty of our universe. That our ancestors named the different qualities of creation the 'gods' was as accurate and authentic as the naming of the Higgs boson particle. There is a poetic beauty behind all of these things.

While poetry is not true in any rational way, it reveals truths inaccessible by literal language. The poetry of Heaney, Yeats or Rilke is not fanciful 'head in the clouds stuff' but visceral, physical and profoundly real. It is the quantum physics of the imagination. Poetry therefore is not for the faint of heart. It is heroic in demanding that you see what cannot be seen and hear what cannot be heard. In terms of fortitude and courage in their quest for truth, the poet is no different from the archaeologist or physicist. The gods will not have their work made manifest by cowards.

Celtic people invoked the gods to give form to what they felt and sensed around them. They sensed a purpose and meaning behind things. They rightly called it the 'otherworld'. Calling forth the gods in order to save their world from nothingness or meaninglessness, these ancient people of Ireland named their gods in order to live life rather than understand it. For these reasons the metaphor of the gods links us to our most basic nature and guards us against literalism. It reminds us of the mythic nature of and our poetic relationship with reality.

It is generally assumed that the Celtic gods of ancient Ireland did not exist and were just a pagan creation to explain away reality. In fact, it was quite the opposite; the gods were entities that did exist and were named in order to reveal reality. This is the view of noted analytic psychologists such as Jung, Campbell and Hillman.

Nowadays it seems as though the gods have wasted away and have been colonised by institutionalised religion, scientific progress and technology. This is not quite so, however. The ancient gods have just taken on new guises and, as a people, we are as animated as ever by a feel for the sacred. We have just repressed and denied it. The ancient gods of Celtic Ireland, mostly local deities, have not been exiled or exterminated but have only changed shape and go under different names such as Happiness or Wealth or Progress.

We are shaped by influences of which we are not even remotely aware. So preoccupied are we with protecting the small square-foot patch of land under our feet that we scarcely lift our heads to feel the wind, breathe the air, or gaze beyond the mountains that shadow us. People live by myths unseen by them, are driven by forces unknown to them, flee from fears that lie beneath them and are searching for something beyond them. It is through this mysterious forest that we travel however much we seek to deny it.

To paraphrase mythologist Joseph Campbell, the ancient Celtic gods have not fled Ireland; they are to be found in their thousands on their way to Croke Park stadium or at the intersection of O'Connell Street and O'Connell Bridge, waiting for the pedestrian lights to change. What he meant by this was that each person standing at those lights is living out a heroic drama, following their personal mythology, drawing their energy and purpose from ancient influences that are beyond their understanding but to which they devote their lives. They honour the ancient gods hidden in the disguise of modern myths because the gods reside within the human soul as much as the natural world. Of course I'm speaking metaphorically here, but, as we shall see, such metaphor lays bare the hard facts of the human enterprise.

The Gods are Present

If our national story were a fable it would say that we have been under a two thousand-year trance from which we strain to awaken. While in this deep sleep we dream of ancient places, heroes and people with magical powers such as Fionn and Cú Chulainn. We toss and turn as a nation with visions of the sea and ancient gods, of ourselves as warriors and saints. Our dreams would be illuminated by brightly coloured animals, wild monks, Celtic Crosses, standing stones and the stone circles of sacred places. We are often half awake, getting glimpses of who we are, and we dream of riding a wild horse across the sea to a mystical land, or find ourselves trapped in the form of a swan or salmon at the edge of some distant lake. In our exile from ourselves and our real identity, we are Grainne hiding among the hedgerows of Ireland, or the broken-hearted Deirdre of the Sorrows.

Like the Tuatha Dé Dannan, the people of the Goddess Danu who departed the physical land of Ireland to the mystical other-world, our Celtic gods have had to give way to the myth of progress, technology or science. Like the Tuatha Dé Danann, the gods have not fled or died away; they reside just behind the veil of external reality. They are your lost voice, your deepest longings and your soul. They reside in your inner cast of characters; they are the gods of your family tree that still inhabit the inner rooms of your memory. They are to be found in the external world too, at sporting occasions, family celebrations and seminal events in the life of a family or community.

Their voice or cry for recognition also emerges in the distress and suffering of people, in anxiety, depression, stress and abuse. Our psychological symptoms are our cries for healing. The epidemic of depression, for example, is the gods' way of telling us that something is wrong, that something in the soul is not aligned. The symptom is a cry from the eternal powers and entities that sustain human life. Psychological symptoms are the voice of the gods telling you that something is not right.

Mythology and Enchantment is Now

To consider mythology a thing of the past is a mistake. We still live by modern myths that are barely visible to us. We are arrogantly convinced that we live by reason, science and logic when in fact we live by forces we do not even begin to comprehend. Just think of the miracle of your own body. The ways in which the brain and body function are, quite simply, jaw-dropping and beyond miraculous.

If you were fearlessly honest you would admit that you live by a hotchpotch of personal spells, secret superstitions, personal beliefs, naive hopes and motivations that inspire you to live a purposeful and heroic life.

Of this we can be certain: in five thousand years' time people will look back at us in the twenty-first century, intrigued by our ancient beliefs and myths and see the remnants of our world as clues to our religious dispositions. Yet where you stand you are as certain of yourself as Stone Age, Neolithic, Mesolithic, Celtic and early Christian people ever were. Everyone feels strangely confident in his or her mythology and it is right that this is so. Yet they never quite grasp its archaic base. Science itself is a mythology; a belief in the necessity of human progress and that science can provide it. Scientists, too, are driven by an existential drive to seek out meaning and knowledge. If you think about it, the belief in science is itself non-scientific.

If you imagine that the gods support you, you can let go a little of your need to justify and prove yourself, your need to control your life and the feeling that you must be responsible for everything. In an uncomplicated and poetic manner, you can imagine the gods in ways that can release you from captivity. It is like hearing the mantra 'Everything is going to be okay' or 'All will be well.'

Given our predicament – inhabiting a mystery we do not comprehend and a life we do not control – we have a choice. We can set ourselves up to direct fate as a little god. Or we can re-imagine the gods as a metaphor for the ancient entities, energies and presences that express the character of a universe that is beyond us. So when you experience 'god' it is like seeing a whale breaking the surface of the sea. Something breaks through. The awe we feel when we see an animal in the wild, even if it is just a hare standing in a morning field, is a glimpse of the gods. Your heart rises up because it longs for a glimpse of the Divine, and in those moments, something is revealed to you. In this way the ancient Celtic gods are ours too. To associate the gods with religion rather than with the poetic intuition of the person is to miss the point. Do not ask if God exists; ask to which god have you become devoted?

We Are Sustained By Invisibilities

Everyday life is sustained and enabled by what Heaney called the invisible 'domain of the imagined'. We exist within two dimensions of reality and we must find a way of keeping a foot in both the matter-of-fact and the imagined. Behind both realities lies an invisible world. One is of sub-atomic quantum energies that hold the universe together and the other is of the inner psychic world that silently guides our life. Together, these invisible forces shape and animate how we live in the world, from the dimensions of space and time to the existential quartet of helplessness, anxiety, insignificance and terror. From the passionate imagination, desire and heroism that energise us, to the pulse, heartbeat, breath and miraculous internal functioning of our body. We swim in a sea of invisible currents that govern our lives. We walk our world under the gravitational pull of unseen forces.

Our everyday life is held together by the vertical values, virtues and entities. In the same way that the physical world is glued together by sub-atomic energies, our psychological life is driven by the vertical unseen myths and beliefs that reassure us: the fantasies that fuel erotic love; the attachment that binds parent to child; the abstractions that take us to war; the imagined offences that cause domestic violence; the affection that draws us together; the narrative to which we belong. They are all unseen. These are our gods.

If we were in ancient Ireland, all these things would be gods. They would be symbolised in rituals, stone circles, standing stones and identified as such. Water, for example, was not just a physical thing – it was identified as a god. In Celtic times nature itself was its own statue, altar or church. It is still the case.

We need a language that appreciates these invisible things and helps us keep a foot in both worlds. Often this has been the language of poetry, music, art, culture, dance or sport. Inspirational, redemptive and consoling, they are our bridges between the vertical and horizontal worlds. Therefore, simple events like a visit to the theatre, experiencing a winter storm, or hearing a poem can reveal the unseen. There are moments in life when, without words, the horizontal and vertical worlds connect. Here you find an invisible and deeply felt resonance, which seems to call forth something in you that you didn't know was there. Our 'Guardian Spirits' exist in real ways that are almost beyond description, but they dwell in the invisible world and touch us at the burning points of life.

The Invisible

The big questions that rumble on in the back of our minds dwell on the gap between the visible and invisible, between the vertical and horizontal realities. How we bridge this gap is the essential question and because it is so essential to our life, we are drawn to experiences that channel the unseen into the seen world. This can be as simple as the exhilaration experienced in attending a sporting occasion, singing in a choir, or dancing alone in your own kitchen when everyone's gone to bed!

Grief also bridges the gap. When someone close to us dies, our grief causes us to recognise the invisible bond that connected us to them and how the meaning of that relationship lies beneath the soil of the visible. Because of this, Rumi could say, 'Everything you see has its roots in the unseen world.'

Poetic words reveal these things because they have a softer sensibility, one that can appreciate the character of invisible things. They allow you to notice the urgency of the vertical life in which we are embedded. So, whether it recognises itself as such or not, a feeling for the sacred is a psychological necessity.

The Abandoned God

Years ago you abandoned God
at the roadside
leaving her like a stray dog
tied to a tree
in the damp countryside of the heart.
Turning away from her sorrowed eyes
you followed the horizontal road
down the cul-de-sac of progress.
Perhaps if you walk backwards
to that decision,
You'd find she still waits,
cold and hungry,
but ears cocked and tail wagging,
And perhaps you will recognise
who it was you left behind:
It was you.

The Original Religious Reflex

If we strip away the dogmas of the world religions and expose the original impulse from which they were formed, we find that it is a natural and essential reflex; a reflex that emerges from a person's felt insignificance and helplessness and makes them a condition of their accord with nature. In religious terms their vulnerability becomes a condition of their salvation or redemption.

Religion is responsible for many social evils across the world because it emphasises difference between people and that difference becomes the basis of sectarianism and prejudice. However, this is a social and political perversion of the original and universal human religious reflex that joins people together. When the earliest human tribes first came together in groups it was not just to maximise productivity and efficiency, it was also to engage in archaic prayer, to join in rituals of gratitude, of sacred reverence and of coming together as a community to share in their existential dependence on the gods.

This original reflex related to fear and gratitude, awe and terror, humility and appreciation. Humanity cried out in grief or dread and sought comfort, consolation, possibility, hope and courage. In the act of crying out, something within the heart shifted ever so slightly. It was a response to the majesty, beauty, power and mystery of nature. The responses of gratitude and fear took the human person beyond him or herself towards the entities on which humanity depended. They metaphorically called these natural forces their gods, which made complete sense. In this uncomplicated *feeling* there was hope – a feeling for something other than the self.

As already discussed, the choice is not whether you live in reality or in illusion – it is what level of enchantment you use to engage with the world. This, again, is not any flight of fancy. In very real ways it can, for example, influence how you behave in your own home. A father who is humble, vulnerable and respectful of others lives at a different level from one who is arrogant, self-righteous and degrading of others. The levels of enchantment that both men live by are very different. The latter is geared towards self-justification, the former towards humility.

The Gods of Sport

To understand human nature you just have to attend any major sporting occasion and instead of watching the game, watch the crowd. Revealed there will be everything you need to know about humanity. Sport allows the spectator and player to experience and participate in something that is not possible in ordinary everyday life. It is more than entertainment, more than distraction, more than just a game.

If you take it totally literally, sport is entirely meaningless. In a purely objective sense, whether one country is better than another country at kicking a piece of pig-skin into a rectangular box with a net is unimportant. You can only understand the passion that surrounds it when you realise that sport is a symbolic activity. It is a theatre in which are acted out aspects of the human predicament that can be expressed only in a symbolic and dramatic way.

When you consider how often you rush to the television to see a last-minute goal, a set point, a crucial putt, a 21-yard free, an unexpected try, or a penalty shoot-out, you will appreciate that something quite extraordinary is happening to you. Nothing in life awakens people's passion and interest like sport. Adults will remember sporting occasions from their childhood like nothing else. They will recall All-Ireland Finals and World Cups as if they were yesterday. They will recall their own success as players – goals they scored, games they won and medals they secured. What is it about sport that has an old man crying and saying that the day his club won the county final was the best day of his life? What is it about sport that can have a nation convulsed in anticipation over something that, objectively speaking, is unimportant? It is because humankind needs to act out the invisible drama of life in symbolic ways. Like ancient Celtic festivals and rituals, sport allows human intensity, passion, emotion and truth to be expressed in the form of a theatrical drama.

While the gods, or fate, hold our destiny in their hands, sport is an arena where we can experience a victory that is not quite available to us in real life. In sport we can invest our deepest longing for victory over that which threatens to defeat us. We can temporarily experience the thrill, relief and excitement of winning in the end, of overcoming fate, of being victorious against mortality. For a short time after victory in sport we experience the exhilaration of what it is like to be ultimately victorious in life. When grown men and women, old people and children roar and cheer with a passion seen nowhere else in human life, you know that it taps into this vital longing in the human psyche. We are all striving to 'do it', to win, to overcome, to defeat the impotence that threatens us, to achieve something and to be a somebody. Sport offers us the possibility to experience this! And what a wonderful feeling it is to shout and cheer after a game and cry, 'We did it! We did it!' Though we rarely see it as such, this enacted victory compensates for the many defeats that threaten to overwhelm us. That is the real victory – the feeling that 'We did it!'

This is what makes sport so wonderful. It can temporarily relieve people of all the possible defeats that threaten their lives. In the moments of sporting victory the depressed are no longer depressed, the anxious are freed of anxiety and the worried are relieved of their burden. Sport is magnificent because it creates an artificial drama within which we experience this possible victory. Through sport we transcend reality and become more than what we are. Life becomes enchanted and, for a short while at least, we know what it is to fly.

Ancient Celtic Festivals Enacted in our Stadiums

To mark the ancient Celtic festivals of the seasons, communities gathered to celebrate, to open the tombs and portals to the gods, to realise their dependency on those gods and on a life bigger than their tribal squabbles. The unawakened mind looks back on those rituals and describes them as pagan, ignorant, and little more than superstition. But to do so is to miss the essential nature of life and to fail to see how today we engage in the same ritual life, just in different forms. At sporting occasions, rock concerts and social gatherings, for example, we are in the service of something beyond the self. As people we are no different from our ancestors ten thousand years ago. Sport is now bigger than the ancient Celtic traditions, but the same eternal hunger to experience humanity's symbolic victory remains. We might call it 'our team', but at a physical and emotional level, it is the gods we follow.

It is a great shame that people are not fully aware of the ancient tribal rituals they are participating in when they attend large group occasions or celebrations. However, at a non-verbal, primal level, people know what to do, how to behave and what it symbolises. When the All Blacks perform the haka before a rugby game it is the last vestige of a reminder of what sport is all about. When I hear crowds jeering the ritual they are failing to experience the sacred element in their own sport. This is because how you meet victory or defeat is more important than winning or losing, than life or death. This is why athletes respect rules and abhor cheating. To win or lose with integrity and honour is to be redeemed and have succeeded as a champion. Cheating is abhorred because it defeats the entire noble purpose of the exercise. Without honour there is no sport.

The Value of Physical Exercise

Young people have enormous natural physical and psychological energy, aggression and combativeness. And sport offers them the experience of being absorbed in the passion of life – of letting anxiety, terror, inadequacy and helplessness fade away. Symbolically, sport is a fight for life. The organised aggression and intense passion exhilarate everyone, both spectator and participant. If you read the Táin symbolically, not literally, what it tells you is that you must engage in a series of battles with your inner adversaries – to the death if needs be – and in so doing, you shall prevail. On the sporting field we enact the greatest defeats and victories in life and thus symbolically rise above the occasion. Win or lose, if we do so with the integrity of a Celtic warrior, there is still the victory of giving our life to a cause greater than our own – to the team or to the core values of the sport itself. It is better to lose with dignity than to win with dishonour.

When the body is pushed to its limits, we experience a physical and somewhat mystical ecstasy. Our peak experiences in life are often related to occasions of physical performance, endurance or intensity. At our physical limit, we can feel the demands of the external world fade away and can arrive at our own centre, where our anxieties drop to zero, so in tune are we with our body. And if you exert yourself with a purpose, it can take you to new levels. It is a metaphor for life.

Chapter 13

Mind-Flight

And even if you can't shape your life the way you want,
at least try as much as you can
not to degrade it
by too much contact with the world.

C.P. Cavafy, 'As Much As You Can'

Beyond Mindfulness

In recent times we have seen an exponential increase in the interest in mindfulness as a way of dealing with life. It is an uncomplicated, gentle and profound way to deal with anxiety, stress and depression. I am a believer in mindful meditation, though like most people I do not practise it as much as I would like.

In Ireland, however, people do not need to look to the West or the East to appreciate the value of the meditative life. Rooted in its history and identity is something of equal relevance to the world. I speak about Ireland's extraordinary monastic tradition as a model of mindfulness. It arose spontaneously from our prehistoric Neolithic tradition, our Celtic spirituality and our early Christian monasticism, and has shown us something that mindfulness does not: the ability of the human mind to be not just in the 'here and now' but also in the 'there and then' and to elevate itself above its circumstances. In our ancient traditions this was characterised by a fearless embracing of the brutal and tragic circumstances of life while cultivating a feeling for the transcendent and the enchantment of life-affirming illusion. Mind-Flight refers to the way the human mind elevates itself above and beyond the limitations of physical existence, situations and time. As we have seen, this has developed through necessity and been made possible by imagination. Mind-Flight is a summary of the provinces of enchantment we have talked about in this book. It is the way of enchantment.

The ability of the human mind to fly has enabled the development of culture, civilisation, religion and art. More important, it has enabled ordinary humans beings to rise to the occasion of life itself and to make something enchanted out of the everyday and something marvellous out of the mediocre. Take as an example a simple birthday celebration for a small child and what it means to his or her self-esteem and place in the world. It is so commonplace that we forget what it means and how it elevates both the child and their family. If you can think of why a birthday celebration ever became a ritual you will realise what it means in terms of life, death, vulnerability and a sense of the sacred. It is just one of hundreds of little ways in which we raise each other up out of the ordeal of life.

Arising from the state of emergency created by consciousness itself, Mind-Flight was built on humanity's drive to exist for something beyond itself. In these ways it has been essential to human evolution and development. It is a direct response to the terror of existence and the existential quartet of inadequacy, insignificance, anxiety and helplessness. More than that, however, it has been a salvaging and embellishment of the sublime experience of being alive. The human mind discovered it was not trapped within the limits of the body and external reality; it could imagine what did not exist, it could transcend circumstance, it could fly in ways that are, when fully appreciated, quite magical. We have looked at some of the ways we do this through heroism, imagination, enchantment, transcendence, immanence and poetry. These are the stepping stones that help us negotiate the sweeping, relentless currents of the river of life.

In these interrelated and overlapping ways, we take flight within the gravitational pull of reality and while we cannot ever escape that reality, we can rise above it through the ways we awaken it, embellish it and add to it in a deeply human way. We awaken the human heart and nudge sleeping reality from its indifference.

Ireland has something in its origins, mythology and psyche that is deeply spiritual, redemptive, poetic and imaginative and which stands shoulder to shoulder with anything from the East or West. The evidence of it lies in the ancient Mesolithic, Celtic and Neolithic monastic history.

Flight in Mythology

From the beginning of recorded history, the theme of flight can be found in myth, legend, art, literature and organised religion. Almost every culture has its own version of angels, flying humans, winged horses and dragons, as well as flying carpets and chariots. The world's folklore is replete with stories of soaring gods and flying heroes who, unlike humans, are able to navigate the sky. Symbolic figures and fantasy creatures representing flight abound, frequently taking the form of human figures equipped with wings; when Oisin went to Tir na nÓg, he flew there by winged horse. The idea of flight suggests freedom and in most cultures connotes supernatural power. The ability of birds to navigate air, land and sea meant they were regarded in mythology as divine messengers; like the dove that returned to the Ark with the branch of hope, birds have the ability to traverse worlds, time and calamities. They were bearers of prophecy and truth regarding fortune or weather.

In Greek mythology the ability to fly was symbolic of godly powers. The power of flight was considered the domain of the immortals. Pegasus is a winged horse that played a part in several legends of the Greek mythology; the Greek myth of Daedalus and Icarus is the classic legend of aeronautics; and Nike served as an angel or messenger of the gods. The belief that Greek gods possessed the power of flight and could span both time and distance at will was well established. In *Portrait of the Artist as a Young Man,* Joyce names his central character Stephen Dedalus after the Greek hero; he created the wings of his art and through them he learned to fly. In night dreams the ability to fly is usually associated with release, peace and a sense of being set free of the chains than bind oneself to the world and one's problems. I'm sure that you have had a dream of flying that you found be beautiful, reassuring and uplifting. Therefore, through Mind-Flight we rise above our earthly troubles to be free and closer to the gods. We gain a new perspective on life.

Mind-Flight in Ancient Ireland

The extraordinary monastic movement that swept through Ireland and Europe in the fifth and sixth centuries was an astonishing cultural example of this flight of the human mind, heart and soul. In their search for something 'beyond', Irish monks set up monasteries of meditation, prayer and learning that were to alter the course of civilisation and elevate the human spirit. These early monks sought out a way of life, prayer and meditation that is a dramatic revelation of the human need for heroic transcendence. The stories of people such as Columcille, Columba, Brendan, Enda, Fionán, Kevin and hundreds of others are the living embodiment of this quite heroic flight of the mind.

Fionán set up the extraordinary hermitage on Skellig Michael, Columba founded his monastery on Iona, Enda set sail for the Aran Islands to establish a place of prayer and learning there, Brendan embarked on a pilgrimage to new worlds, Kevin founded Glendalough by seeking out a hermit's life of prayer – these were all spiritual trailblazers who sought to leave the horizontal world of status and conflict to seek the vertical otherworld of mindfulness and learning and to live for something more than the here and now.

As mentioned in the Introduction to this book, the Skelligs are a symbol of this will and desire. They are a magnificent illustration of the ability of the human mind to bring all of heaven down into a small stone cell on top of a rock in the midst of a raging ocean – to expand outwards into the universe to inhabit the stars and to see one's little hermit's life from above. This is not fanciful make-believe. This ancient, courageous flight of the mind illustrates how we make life passionate, how we light the flame of human expansiveness and set free the eagle of freedom.

This Mind-Fight is how we are supposed to live. With our feet planted firmly in the earth we can look to the sky and allow the mind to fly free of its mortal imprisonment. We know intuitively that this is what we need when we are depressed, anxious, stressed or bereaved. The Skelligs are the ultimate example of Mind-Flight. Go to the Skelligs. Remember who you are. Discover the ancient in you.

Mind-Flight in Everyday Life

While mindfulness is staying in the here and now, Mind-Flight is the mental levitation or flight to an elevated third dimension. We engage in this form of mental flight in a myriad of ordinary ways as we tap into hope, courage, determination or desire. It is the vertical release from the here and now and a lifting outwards and upwards with hope rather than fear. Fear can make Mind-Flight an escape from reality; hope makes it an embracing of reality. Mind-Flight closes the circle between the now and then and draws an all-embracing arc over the time-line of one's past, present and future.

Mind-Flight has been a universal activity across cultures since the dawn of humankind. Ever day, in ordinary, unremarkable ways, we levitate using humour, sport, music, dance or altered states of consciousness. We do it with daydreaming, play, anticipation and reminiscing. We experience it in prayer, wonder, awe, poetry and in the feeling that we belong to something bigger than ourselves. We do it when we affirm ourselves, or when we visualise our future self in ways that inspire us. We do it in positive daydreaming, recollection, mind travelling, night dreaming, or mindful walking. It is evoked when we laugh and play and awaken the endorphins of childhood.

We also have to do it when dealing with tragedy, as we cling to some thread of hope that we have little right to hold on to; when coping with grief by patiently waiting for its weight to lift; when dealing with temporary frustration in the service of a goal that lies beyond it; when living for an invisible beyond that redeems and rescues the present moment; when dissociating from trauma by being able to be out of one's body and separating one's soul from the pain; and when re-imagining our life in a way that elevates an invisible personal narrative that has been smothered beneath a dominant one that diminished us.

When we praise young children their *sense of themselves* is lifted, bringing a smile of relief to their faces that allows them to feel *I am more than I thought I was.* Affirmation and encouragement are eaten up by little children, hungry as they are for any kind of a lift that helps them climb a little higher out of the sea of ordinariness in which they threaten to drown.

Grandparents intuitively know this better than parents and go out of their way to make grandchildren feel that little bit special. This proclaims a truth beyond words – that the food the human heart needs is one that lifts the heart out of the ordinary, out of the here and now, to a plane above mortality. This is the unspeakable truth, and words like, 'You are the most delightful little girl I know' are the magic enchantment that elevates the human heart and enables it to get up off the ground. The wings of the little child flutter a little and for a moment she can fly.

My mother sent a wonderfully simple text to my little daughter that read:

> For Ciara: ☺
> Thank you so much for my chocolate cupcake.
> It was so nice.
> I had it last night for my supper and it was lovely. ☺
> You are great. Thanks again.
> Love, Nan

The blessings of a grandparent are invaluable and enduring. This is such a simple text, but when you feed the human heart the child lifts up ever so slightly and is sustained by a silent inner charm or enchantment. Both the affirmation of the grandparent and the appreciation of the grandchild occur in the invisible currency of the human spirit and are as real and vital as the cupcake that was made and eaten.

All the acts of love shown towards another person lift them up out of the mud of everyday toil. The hidden purpose of the five 'currencies' of love (emancipation, affirmation, affection, protection and encouragement) is to elevate the person's heart above the surface of their life. These simple acts of kindness lift the person up, hold the bird heart of the other and nudge it into flight. To say to someone *I set you free to be who you are* is to foster a flight of the heart. To say *Go for it, I support and am behind you in whatever you try to do* is to foster the flight of the anxious heart. To say *I want to be close to you, to care for you tenderly* is to relax the lonely heart of another and allow it to levitate. And so on. Love lifts the other towards the light and rejects the option of cynicism and rejection that diminish the other and drive them further into the ground zero of the unimagined life.

In contrast, when we experience any of the currencies of rejection (control, criticism, abuse, disregard and alienation) we fall, we sink into mortality and, metaphorically at least, we die. So we see that love is the elevation of the human heart; rejection is its degradation. We can either elevate or diminish the other. To the person who is without imagination or the aesthetic of awakening, there is no love, no elevation, no magic. Love that has one foot in the enchanted world and one foot in the mortal is real because it engages life in a literal and symbolic way.

The Kite of Hope

The ability to 'take mental flight' says that no matter what your circumstances, no matter how imprisoned you are by life, a part of you can break free. This is not make-believe avoidance but a real lifeline that runs, like the string of a kite, from the prison cell to the sky outside. Imagine that a string runs from your wrist to a little red kite that rises ahead of you and carries you forward. It is the kite tied to the wrist of the refugee walking the mountainside, the woman waiting to escape an abusive relationship. It is the kite of hope that keeps you going and takes you up and out of yourself towards a better place.

Our ability for Mind-Flight represents hope and freedom. It allows the imprisoned, the scared and the lonely to rise above their circumstances. The little girl who discovers that the magic of reading books saves her from the domestic abuse in which she is trapped. The young boy whose dreams for the future enable him to climb up out of poverty and be successful.

Mind-Flight is a prayer, a grounded fantasy that elevates the soul. It is an incantation. It is an awareness that we are vertical beings inhabiting a horizontal world, or that we are horizontal beings with a vertical purpose. It is leverage for those who want a better life, the motivation for those who want to succeed, the consolation for those who are bereaved and the gateway through which one liberates the self.

So caught was Yeats by his own mortality that he longed for Mind-Flight, as expressed in his classic poem 'Sailing to Byzantium', Byzantium being a fictitious city to which he fancied he could take flight. He opens his poem with the lines 'That is no country for old men', where 'An aged man is but a paltry thing, A tattered coat upon a stick'. It is as if, by writing about the themes that I explore in this book, he is confronting death and his decay. He wants to be taken away to where he is no longer tied to his own body, which he feels is a dying creature who exclaims:

> Consume my heart away; sick with desire
> And fastened to a dying animal
> It knows not what it is; and gather me
> Into the artifice of eternity.

And the poem finds some resolution in Mind-Flight as he sings 'Of what is past, or passing, or to come.'

Celtic Meditation

In the personal development groups I facilitate, I use a flight meditation to allow people to lift up out of themselves and look down at their lives with compassion. Most people find this simple meditation helps release the self from the ties that bind it. For example, as you sit there reading this, imagine looking at yourself as if from an elevated position. See what you notice when you do this and observe how it alters your feelings about yourself every so slightly. If you look at yourself as if from above, what do you notice?

Mind-Flight in Childhood

Mind-Flight leaves its fingerprints all over your childhood. If you think back to what excited, interested and affected you as a child you will recall experiences of mental flight and elevation. Your memories probably include pretend-play, dreams of who you wanted to be, heroes and how they inspired you and an inner imaginary life known only to you; an inner imagination that continues right through to the present day.

The moral development of children is also fascinating. It shows that the child is able to imagine concepts like fairness and goodness that exist as abstract concepts but do not exist in the physical world. In a similar way children imagine and believe in a lot of things for which they have no evidence, like the planets or places around the world. These are little examples of the myriad ways in which the mind of the child can 'fly'.

We hold memories of the past in a storehouse of imagination that gives us a very real sense of self. We can draw up an image of the place we grew up in that 'brings us back', even though we do not move one inch. This is the wonder of imagination and Mind-Flight. If I ask you to imagine the house you grew up in and to walk between its rooms and remember the feel of it, you can do this at will in a way that can evoke a host of sensations. This is the magic of Mind-Flight – that you can take this journey back in time without moving a limb.

Yeats evoked this metaphor of flight to another land in this melodious and haunting verse from 'The Stolen Child':

> Come away, O human child!
> To the waters and the wild
> With a faery, hand in hand,
> For the world's more full of weeping than you can
>   understand.

Emancipation through Mind-Flight

We levitate in ways that enable us to endure suffering or distress. We expand outwards as a form of mental emancipation. At the simplest level, just notice how ninety per cent of your day is spent in problem-focused daydreaming – thinking about things you are going to do or figuring out how you are going to solve little problems. All of this is happening because of your ability to contemplate a future situation, and to engage in foresight, all of which is imagined.

Self-consciousness itself, the acute awareness of what is happening at any given time, is the sensation of being slightly outside of what is happening and being able to look in. The simple thought, as you drive along a scenic route, that 'This is beautiful, I love this!' is an elevation above an experience and witnessing it at a different level. In mindfulness you experience it without that elevation; with Mind-Flight you levitate ever so slightly and are in relationship with the world rather than being immersed in it.

Mind-Flight

As we have seen, the response of the individual and society to the human predicament has been extraordinary, magnificent and heroic. The response of the human psyche to death, mortality, helplessness and the majesty of creation has been inspirational. It is seen in our urge to build civilisations, to establish significance where none would appear possible, to conceive of things that do not exist in the world and to create self-esteem in the face of the indifference of life. They are all examples of how the human mind has learned to fly towards the heavens while tied to the ground zero of earth.

The heroic urge to live for some imagined value is Mind-Flight; the religious reflex of archaic and modern human beings to give life a meaning and purpose that it does not have is Mind-Flight; the ability of the human artist to carve beauty out of the hard marble of life's indifference is Mind-Flight; the ability of a person to imagine all sorts of things that do not exist in reality is to lift the marvellous out of the mundane; the ability of the human person to cast an enchanting spell over an ordinary life that turns it into an extraordinary odyssey is Mind-Flight; the virtue of hope and the ability of any individual to live for something when circumstances seem hopeless is Mind-Flight; the ancient and innocent quality of transcendence that is buried in the ancient religions is Mind-Flight; the levitations of the mind that attend mindfulness, meditation and prayer are all Mind-Flight; and, not least of all, sporting occasions, movies and literature that all elevate the human above and beyond the ordinariness of life make something magical happen and are all Mind-Flight. All of these things involve the elevation of the human mind above and beyond literal reality.

Mind-Flight is not just a technique; rather, it is a reflex and a heroic response to limitation, a sacred savouring of possibility and a transformation of literal reality. Mind-Flight shows our extraordinary ability to turn a tiny space into a palace, an unexpected misfortune into an opportunity, a disability into a blessing. Adversity causes Mind-Flight by forcing a person to redefine themselves and transcend its literal effects – an opportunity never afforded by good fortune.

> Come to the edge.
> We might fall.
> Come to the edge.
> It's too high!
> COME TO THE EDGE!
> And they came,
> and we pushed,
> And they flew.
>
> *Christopher Logue, 'Come to the Edge'*

Changing Perspective

Our language is littered with words and phrases describing the ability of the human mind to see things from another perspective. Common everyday phrases like 'taking another look', 'seeing things in a new light', 'seeing with the mind's eye,' or 'changing one's perspective' use the metaphor of sight to describe how one gains this new perspective. Though sight is not involved at all, the metaphor is intuitive as it fits in with other metaphors of 'rising above' or transcendence, which are positions from which one sees things differently.

Fantasies of being able to go to another world fill our everyday imagination. Children's stories are replete with references to other 'lands' and nearly always involve some kind of journey to a place where things are seen in a different way – for good or for bad. Ancient myths and legends, too, refer to magical places or events in the 'otherworlds'. Legends such as Fionn

Mac Cumhaill and the Salmon of Knowledge, Oisín in Tir na nÓg, the Children of Lir and Deirdre of the Sorrows are all wonderful stories that mix the tangible world with the world of imagination. One of the hidden messages in all these stories is simply that *things are never as they seem – there is another way to view life.*

Joseph Campbell suggested that the picture of Earth from space was *the* image of the twentieth century and the basis of a new myth regarding the state of humanity. Carl Sagan, the astronomer, spoke poetically about the wonderful image of Earth taken from Jupiter that shows planet Earth to be a 'pale blue dot' in the distant night sky and a dramatic image of our need to have a radically new perspective on our place in the universe.

Mind-Flight and Celtic Spirituality

Celtic and pre-Celtic spirituality is a wonderful tapestry of beliefs, rituals and myths that reveal the profound importance of Mind-Flight and transcendence to the human enterprise. Since the first heartbeat of self-consciousness, humankind has sought to give symbolic expression to the vertical life, to respond in some transcendent way to the limits of helpless mortality, to bear witness to the fact that things are so much more than they seem and to illustrate that there is another world within which we exist. This is best expressed through symbol, myth, ritual, poetry, art, music and the original and innocent religious reflex. Our Celtic spirituality, literature, traditions, sacred places and myths express all these things. Illumination as a technique in Celtic art, and seen at its best in the Book of Kells, is symbolic of our desire to shine light into dark places, find meaning where there is little, climb out of the mud of self-oppression and fly.

Coming Back Down to Earth

> Soar, don't settle for earth
> and sky – soar to Orion.
>
> *Shmuel Hanagid, 'Soar, Don't Settle'*

From Mind-Flight, we must all come back down to earth. Yet we return with the vision of having seen things from above, of a little bit of magic. This is how we create an enchanted life. We have to drift back down from the sky to the earth of human affairs. And whatever our circumstances, worries or grief, the crucial point is that this capacity to rise above things is ever present. It is our essential humanity.

It is not a technique or trick, it is the way humans have evolved after the first heartbeat of self-awareness. This is how we endure, how we cheerfully carry our burdens, how we have built our cities and towns. We sing as we die because we see something that is beyond. Cut open the brain and this something is not there. Take a picture and it is not there. It is not visible, yet it is the soul of the human heart. It is the small bird of the self that can fly free from worries and, like a skylark, sing of things not yet seen.

There are of course times in life when instead of being elevated, you are pulled down deep into the earth, covered by the heavy soil of stress, or embedded fully in the darkness of loss. At such times, talk of elevation is neither right nor sympathetic.

> Yet, almost despite yourself and your abject
>   circumstance,
> the faint heartbeat of hope
> still gives off a distant reverberation
> still gasps for breath
> and sends green shoots up
> to break the soil of sorrow,
> if only to just keep itself alive
> while it waits
> and waits
> and waits
> with your grief.

When sunk deep in the earth, you are in the realm of soul. When rising up from it, you are in the realm of spirit. Spirit grows from the earth of the soul. It is not the other way around. Soul knows the suffering and grief of life and makes spirit possible and necessary.

The Solace of Prayer

> To pray unselfconsciously with overflowing speech
> For this soul needs to be honoured with a new dress
>   woven
> From green and blue things and arguments that cannot
>   be proven.

> *Patrick Kavanagh, 'Canal Bank Walk'*

My dear mother, now in her eighties, has for some time been carrying everywhere with her a little prayer card that says: 'Lord, I surrender myself to You. Take care of everything.' A cynic might consider this little prayer a form of delusion, naive hope, or child-like religiosity, but it is in fact courageous, honest and deeply human. My mother has described how this simple and modest prayer gives her solace, hope and relief.

Her prayer reveals everything that is exceptional and magnificent about the human person. It is this: she experiences every day the crude brutality of life because everything is slipping away from her – her vision, hearing, strength, health, independence. However, she does not allow it to bring her down into anything close to a fatalistic despair. In surrendering to an image of God and in locating that God beyond her, she keeps alive a light of hope, faith and cheerfulness. People like her are an inspiration because of the way they deal with life's cruel circumstances, such as ailing health or chronic pain. Instead of sinking, she struggles to fly – and when she fails to lift off, she tries again. I called one evening and before she could see me I watched her in the garden and afterwards wrote this:

On a summer evening
she is in the green garden
among the lush leaves
tossing crumbs
to the tamed blackbird
that hops close to her chair.

When I look out the window
she is whispering happily
to her winged friend,
and I see her lifting with him
when he takes holy flight.

By way of our human enchantment, we do not delude ourselves but we play a trick on life itself. We dance when life expects us to submit. We sing when life expects us to moan. We laugh when life expects us to be dour. We fly when life expects us to fall. This flight is part magical enchantment and part brutal reality, but to the degree that it elevates us from suffering, it not only succeeds, it transforms us.

Prayer, because it is an instance in which the human person wants to rely on a centre outside him or herself, is an extraordinary existential event. We pray to cope with physical reality, suffering or mortality. And whether or not that centre outside us exists in reality is not the point. In fact, even if we conclude that the gods do not exist, the plea from the heart is no less genuine and its effects are no less real. What moves and inspires me about genuine prayer is how it eases suffering, inspires the person and fosters humility. A prayer is an acknowledgement of so many things and on so many levels it can liberate us from self-absorption, guilt, self-justification, obsessive control and narcissism. Everything I have spoken about in this book is acknowledged in a wordless way by a simple prayerful gesture or action.

Prayer comes before any belief in god and, for me at least, does not require it. The cry of the rabbit caught by a hound will haunt you not because it is just a cry of pain, but because it is a pleading for relief. Prayer is not an act of delusion (as some might argue), nor is it a rational act. It is a cry of imagination and inspired illusion. This kind of inspired illusion is reality-enhancing. It enables us to jump across the rapids of life, from one stepping-stone to the next, with faith and hope.

Postscript

Na Daoine Draíochta

The Enchanted People

Consolation, Hope and Faith

There are so many questions for which the dominant social professions such as science, politics, or medicine have no answer. The questions posed by a mother at the graveside of her eight-year-old son; by an abused woman battered in front of her children; by a good man who has lost everything to the recession; by a father who discovers he has an aggressive form of motor neurone disease; by a young man who wants to end his life; or by a child who just wants the abuse to stop. These are all situations for which science can offer no consolation. Neither politics nor our dominant professions have the will or wherewithal to embrace life's unavoidable cruelty and brutality, or to understand fully the meaning of consolation or transcendence. This is why all meaningful spirituality is a response to suffering – it is about what we do with the anguish of life.

However, just as I cite the examples above, these same people, in these very hopeless positions, may have elevated themselves, found sufficient heroic purchase in their lives to enable them to be not mere victims of life, but to thrive in spite of and because of it. Those who succeed in doing this demonstrate humanity at its absolute best. They show that it is within our gift to salvage some fragment of hope from broken dreams. They bring all of life's eternal mysteries, challenges and hopes to bear on their own unbearable life circumstance. In this way each person struggles with, and partially resolves, the great biblical themes of Life.

Consolation cannot be found in platitudes and sympathies that try to turn us away from life's harshest truths. Instead, it is found in the magical, symbolic, poetic and imagined world that is at times more real than the physical one. As we age, this becomes much more apparent.

We heal ourselves in the rivers of the imagination, we stand under the sky of the dreams we live by. It sounds strange to say something like this, but those who have felt the hammer blows of grief know what it is that consoles them. The poetic imagination does not answer life's questions, but what it does provide is consolation. In life we often need this more than we need answers.

After Nelson Mandela died, Barack Obama said: 'He showed what we can achieve when we are guided by our hopes and not by our fears.' Hope is necessary because our situation is in so many ways quite hopeless. If our situation were not hopeless in some way, we would not need hope. We would march forward with a delusional certainty about our future victory and satisfaction. Faith is necessary because our knowledge is paltry. Hope is necessary because we face the unknown.

Part possibility and part illusion, hope rises up regardless of fatal circumstance and even because of it. Focused not on the here and now, but on the there and then, it is a transcendent faculty – the belief that whatever happens, one will be able for it. Frankl articulated this beautifully when he said that we must not accept what we are, we must strive to be more than we are and in so doing we become who we are capable of becoming. This is Hope – being prepared for more and imagining more than there is. Every person has some degree of hope that enables him or her to endure, from the reformed alcoholic who struggles with sobriety to the old man slowly walking to the doctor's surgery. Faith is a trust that something outside the self sustains the self.

> The tide fills again the rock pools of your heart
> As the moon of the vertical world
> Swings round again and spills the ocean into you
> Wordlessly giving you what you need.

When you live in faith, you do not try to wrestle meaning from horizontal concerns. Instead you hand meaning over to life, to the universe, to an imagined god, or to the will of nature. The vertical person gratefully accepts what happens on the horizontal dimension, because their centre of gravity lies in the vertical one – in a secure faith.

Na Daoine Draíochta

This book was written for the many people who live lives of quiet unseen heroism – those beatific people who make this world a better place through humility and gratitude. Those people who, when you meet them, elevate you by their humility and dignity. They have a way of being that enchants an often unforgiving life with the sparkle of their cheerfulness.

These are people who in Irish folklore were referred to as the enchanted people, *na daoine draíochta*, as my late father used to call them. In myth and folklore stories were told about such people as if they were from another world. However, the stories were really lyrical representations of the necessity of enchantment for ordinary people, for the peasantry of Ireland, as Yeats called them, to help cope with the ordeals of life. In this way many of our stories, myths and legends suggest that there is always a magical ingredient available through which one could experience things a little differently. In ancient Irish fairy tales and legend the *daoine síog* (the fairy people) are really a personification, an illustration, of our potential for an enchanted life.

In this myth and folklore, there is a difference between the real world and the otherworld that is not immediately perceptible. It tells you that everything that is 'here' in the real world is also 'there', but the things that are 'there' are enchanted. All things that are bright in this world are illuminated in the other. A place where according to Irish tradition:

[T]here is more gold in the sun and more silver in the moon ... Everything ... is better by this one wonderful degree, and it is by this betterness you will know that you are there if you should ever happen to get there.

Gerald Benedict, *Celtic Wisdom*

In Irish folklore this truth is told in wonderful, fanciful stories of magic and mystery. However, they are really indirect suggestions about how we must inhabit this world of suffering we call life. This otherworld is really the world that opens up to you when you are wounded by the vulnerability of life. The experiences that open this window to the otherworld are ones you would not ever wish upon yourself – loss, death, tragedy, illness and so on. Yet, in these times of brokenness a light can shine in that illuminates things in yourself that you otherwise would never have seen or known. In these times you become one of the *daoine draíochta*. You realise that life is elevated from its tragic and at times cruel nature by the enchantments of the heart – when the otherworld spills into this one.

The existence of the world and our ability to transcend it is dependent on the beatific and wounded people who can see behind the veil of reality; people who live holy lives, enchant this world, elevate the lives of others and illuminate the path ahead. These people, unaware of their blessed nature, go about their lives with a humility and grace that redeems this harsh world.

As suggested in stories about the fairy people, they are barely visible and do not attract attention. The world depends on them and, dear reader, let me suggest that perhaps you are one of them. Perhaps you walk this world with a tenderness and compassion that goes unseen; perhaps your contribution to the world is greater than you imagine because you have one hand holding back the curtain to the enchanted. In your ordinary life the candle-glow of your being casts a soft light into the dark of the world. Where, as an ancient Irish proverb might suggest: 'The window to the other world is closer than your hand.'

To conclude, let me encourage you and say *slán* thus:

> You stay obsessed with
> Your list of things to do
> And your horizontal victories.
> You are afraid that if you stood vertical in the world,
> dug your bare feet into the damp earth,
> and reached up to the heavens
> that no hand would come to meet you;
> that if you cried, no one would hear.
> But think of this:
> What if an angel took pity on you
> And reaching down
> Gripped your stretching hand.
> What beauty would befall you,
> what grace would fill your heart.
> Put aside your lists,
> feel the grief of the earth,
> reach for the hand of the enchanted.

Bibliography

A jigsaw piece in my life fell into place when I read the towering work of the late anthropologist Ernest Becker. Becker opened a window of wonder for me because of the connection he made between the spiritual life and the terror of death that drives us forward. Those familiar with his work will find his fingerprints throughout these pages. I have also been inspired by the work of mythologist Joseph Campbell, who first came to my attention when I watched his PBS TV series *The Power of Myth* in the USA in the 1980s. His encyclopaedic knowledge of world mythology and his application of it to everyday life was an awesome achievement, and if you have not seen those tapes, I urge you to do so. Others whose work have inspired and affirmed parts of this book include the Irish poet Seamus Heaney, whose descriptions of his own mission affirmed my efforts; and Jungian analyst James Hillman, whose appreciation of the ancient gods, like Campbell's, awakened my own. I am also indebted to various historical writers whose works have opened up elements of ancient Irish history and mythology that otherwise would have remained closed. They include, in particular, historians Brendan Lehane, Eoin Neeson and Jeffrey Gantz, and researchers Carmel McCaffrey, Leo Eaton and Thomas Cahill. To all of these authors I owe a gesture of gratitude. The following represents a list of those writers and others whose work I must salute.

Astley, N. (ed.) (2011), *Being Human*, Bloodaxe, Northumberland, UK.

Astley, N. (ed.) (2003), *Do Not Go Gentle*, Bloodaxe, Northumberland, UK.

Astley, N. and Robertson-Pearch, P., (eds) (2007), *Soul Food*, Bloodaxe, Northumberland, UK.

Becker, E. (1973), *The Denial of Death*, Free Press, New York.

Benedict, G. (ed.) (2008), *Celtic Wisdom: The poetry and prose of a mystic tradition*, Duncoan Baird, London.

Biggs, F. (2014), *Pocket Irish Legends*, Gill & Macmillan, Dublin.

Cahill, T. (1995), *How the Irish Saved Civilization*, Hodder & Stoughton, London.

Campbell, J. (2008), *The Hero with a Thousand Faces*, New World Library, California, USA.

Campbell, I. (1999), *The Hero's Journey*, Element, Dorset, UK.

Castledon, R., (2012), *The Element Encyclopaedia of the Celts*, Harper Collins, London.

De Waal, E. (1996), *The Celtic Way of Prayer*, Hodder & Stoughton, London.

Ellis, P.B. (2003), *A Brief History of the Celts*, Constable & Robinson, London.

Emick, J. (2009), *The Everything Celtic Wisdom Book*, Adams Media, Avon, Massachusetts.

Ferguson, R. (2013), *Life Lessons from Kierkegaard*, Pan Macmillan, London.

Gill, E. and Everett, D. (1997), *Celtic Pilgrimages*, Blandford, London.

Gray, J. (2012), *The Immortalisation Commission*, Penguin, London.

Gantz, J. (1981), *Early Irish Myths and Sagas*, Penguin, London.

Heaney, S. (1995), *The Redress of Poetry*, Faber & Faber, London.

Hillman, J. (1976), *Re-Visioning Psychology*, Harper & Rowe, New York.

Ledwidge, F. (1974), *Francis Ledwidge Complete Poems*, Martin Brian & O'Keefe, London.

Mafi, M. and Kolin, A.M. (2012), *Rumi's Little Book of Life*, Hampton Roads, Vermont.

Michell, S., (2002), *Can Love Last?*, Norton & Co., New York.

McCaffrey, C. and Eaton, L. (2002), *In Search of Ancient Ireland*, New Amsterdam, Chicago.

Neeson, E. (1998, 3rd edn), *Celtic Myths and Legends*, Mercier Press, Cork.

O'Grady, W. (1919), *The Triumph and Passing of Cuchulainn*, Stokes, New York.

Rank, O. (1958), *Beyond Psychology*, Dover, New York.

Solomon, S. *et al.*, (2015), *The Worm at the Cove*, Random House, New York.

Williams, M. and Penman, D. (2011), *Mindfulness*, Piatkus, London.

Yeats, W.B. (2004), *The Book of Fairy and Folk Tales of Ireland*, Bounty, London.